WORLD TRAVELER
GREECE

AAA Publishing
Heathrow, Florida, U.S.A.

Published by the American Automobile Association, 1000 AAA Drive, Heathrow, Florida 32746, in conjunction with NTC/Contemporary Publishing Company, Lincolnwood, Illinois and AA Publishing, Basingstoke, England.

Above: *in the National Gardens, Athens*

Page 1: *the Temple of Apollo at Delphi*

Page 5a: *sunset at Cape Sounion;*
Page 5b: *Greek Easter eggs*

Page15a: *Metéora;*
Page 15b: *golden mask from Mycenae*

Page 27a: *Alexander the Great in Thessaloníki;*
27b: *traditional costume, Métsovo*

Page 91a: *high fashion in Athens;*
91b: *taverna sign*

Page 117a: *Chalkidikí coastline;*
117b: *octopus*

The contents of this publication are believed correct at the time of printing. Nevertheless, the publishers cannot accept responsibility for errors or omissions, nor for changes in details given. We are always grateful to readers who let us know of any errors or omissions they come across, and future printings will be updated accordingly.

Written by Mike Gerrard

Library of Congress Catalog Card Number: on file
ISBN 0–8442–0136–7

Color separation: BTB Digital Imaging, Whitchurch, Hampshire

Printed and bound in Italy by Printer Trento srl

The weather chart on **page 118** of this book is calibrated in °C. For conversion to °F simply use the following formula:

$$°F = 1.8 \times °C + 32$$

Contents

About this Book

Essential *Mainland Greece* is divided into five sections to cover the most important aspects of your visit to Mainland Greece.

Viewing Mainland Greece pages 5–14
An introduction to the mainland by the author.
Features of Mainland Greece
Essence of Mainland Greece
The Shaping of Mainland Greece
Peace and Quiet
Famous of Mainland Greece

Top Ten pages 15–26
The author's choice of the Top Ten places to see in Mainland Greece, each with practical information.

What to See pages 27–90
The four main areas of Mainland Greece, each with its own brief introduction and an alphabetical listing of the main attractions.
Practical information
Snippets of 'Did You Know...' information
4 suggested walks
4 suggested tours
2 features

Where To... pages 91–116
Detailed listings of the best places to eat, stay, shop, take the children and be entertained.

Practical Matters pages 117–24
A highly visual section containing essential travel information.

Maps
All map references are to the individual maps found in the What to See section of this guide.
For example, the Acropolis has the reference ✚ 34C2 – indicating the page on which the map is located and the grid square in which the ancient site is to be found. A list of the maps that have been used in this travel guide can be found in the index.

Greek Placenames
Romanised spellings of Greek names can vary. In placename headings and in the index, this book uses transliterations which follow a recognised convention and which correspond to AA maps. More familiar Anglicised spellings (given in brackets in the headings) are sometinmes used in the text.

Prices
Where appropriate, an indication of the cost of an establishment is given by **£** signs: **£££** denotes higher prices, **££** denotes average prices, while **£** denotes lower charges.

Star Ratings
Most of the places described in this book have been given a separate rating:
✪✪✪ Do not miss
✪✪ Highly recommended
✪ Worth seeing

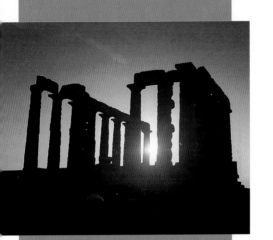

Viewing Mainland Greece

Mike Gerrard's Mainland Greece

Filoxenia

The Greek alphabet may baffle, and spoken Greek may sound like a machine-gun rattle, but the language has one important word in it: *filoxenia*. Difficult to translate, it means both 'stranger' and 'guest' simultaneously. This is the Greek view, and the result may be the drink that arrives unannounced at your table, the bill that has been settled by someone else, and the invitations to sit down, to talk, and to stay.

The Greek Islands have many virtues, one being that they attract the majority of holiday-makers and allow the mainland to remain more purely Greek. The two principal cities of the mainland, Athens and Thessaloníki, could be nowhere else on earth: ancient and modern, vast yet still village-like and both extend a welcome like a hearty slap on the back.

Its landscape, too, is as dramatic as the people who live in it, the people for whom a bus-ride is an emotional event and arm-waving is a way of life. From the Víkos Gorge in the north, the second-longest gorge in Europe, down to the rugged landscapes of the remote Máni, mainland Greece is a region of stunning beauty. It is a land of mountains like the Píndos and Parnassós ranges and Mount Olympus. It is also a land of mountain villages and of attractive lakeside towns, such as Kastoriá and Ioánnina, set like sparkling jewels against blue waters.

For many visitors, the mainland is the home of Classical Greece: history-rich Athens, the running track and ruins at Olympía, the geometrical magic of the theatre at Epídavros and, greatest of all, Delphi, regarded by the ancients as the centre of the universe.

'Know thyself' was the advice of the oracle there in the 6th century BC, and the Greeks do have the relaxed nature of people who are comfortable with themselves: civil but not servile, friendly but not fawning, openly extending the hand of friendship.

The busy little harbour at Marmaras, Chalkidikí

Features of Mainland Greece

Geography

• The Greek mainland comprises 130,000sq km at the southern end of Europe's Balkan Peninsula. There is a mountainous spine to the country, primarily the Píndos range in the north, and as a result only one-third of the land is cultivated.

• The most southerly part of the mainland is the Peloponnese, surrounded by the Aegean Sea. Here the land is slightly less mountainous, but the almost constant visible presence of either mountains or sea gives the Greek mainland a distinctive look.

Religion

The Orthodox religion is very strong in Greece and is practiced by 98% of the population. The remainder comprises a Muslim minority of 1.3% mostly in Thráki (Thrace), Roman Catholics and Jews.

Climate

• Greece is a temperate country, with hot, dry summers and wet, mild winters. Mountain regions can be bitterly cold in winter, while the temperature in Athens can rise to almost 40°C in summer. Spring and autumn are good times to visit.

Population

• Greece's population is approaching 11 million, with one-third living in Athens.

• Over 98% of the population is Greek, the remainder comprising small numbers of Albanians, Jews, Turks, Pomaks and declining numbers of semi-nomadic Vlach and Sarakatsani shepherds.

Languages

• Greek is the official language, but English is widely spoken, and in the tourist areas French, German and Italian, too. In remote areas it is likely that only Greek will be understood.

The sun sets over the port of Vólos, as seen from high on the Pílio peninsula

7

Essence of Mainland Greece

The Greeks are a passionate people: passionate about politics, about religion, about family... about life. At the same time they are phlegmatic and fatalistic: the bus or ferry may be an hour late, but so what? It will come when it comes. To understand these opposite qualities is to begin to get the most out of Greece. Be patient when patience is called for, as it so frequently is, but enjoy life when you can, through food, music, laughter, dance. Enjoy the landscape too. The Greek mainland remains one of Europe's least-known regions: mountains, lakes, gorges, rivers, forests... and, yes, beaches too.

Visitors arrive at the Parthenón (main picture) and (inset) a fine carved head from the Archaeological Museum in Thessaloníki

THE 10 ESSENTIALS

If you only have a short time to visit Mainland Greece, or would like to get a really complete picture of the country, here are the essentials:

• **Visit the Acropolis** (➤ 17), which never disappoints in reality no matter how familiar it may seem to be from photographs and films.

• **Eat by the waterside** – fresh fish, freshly grilled, with a view across the wine-dark seas, is as much a joy on the mainland as on any Greek island.

• **Spend time at Delphi** (➤ 18), preferably early in the morning or late in the day, when the crowds have dispersed. Take your time and you will know that you are in one of the world's magical places.

• **Take a bus ride**. The bus service is excellent, relied upon by much of the population, and if the journey is uneventful the scenery will still delight.

• **Visit a monastery**, whether the grand holy places like Metéora (➤ 24) or Mount Athos (➤ 16), or the more humble retreats. You don't need to be religious, or knowledgeable about Byzantine icons, to appreciate the spirituality.

• **Speak some Greek** and the Greeks will appreciate it. They know their language is difficult for foreigners, and even a simple Greek phrase will often be rewarded with a beaming smile.

• **Explore the mountains**. You will not see the most spectacular parts of the mainland if you don't venture up the zig-zag mountain roads.

• **Linger over a coffee**, as the Greeks do, watching the world go by and feeling your worries slip right away.

• **See Greek dancing**: the best is spontaneous, not organised for tourists, so

keep your fingers crossed and your ears pricked for music.

• **Drink *retsina***, and not till you acquire a taste for it can you say you've acquired a taste for Greece.

Above: *spring blossom and the Varlaám monastery at Metéora*

9

The Shaping of Mainland Greece

c3000 BC
Evidence of first settlements around the Acropolis in Athens.

1700–1600
The emergence of Mycenaean culture on the mainland.

1400
The Acropolis becomes a royal fortress.

1200
Final collapse of Mycenaean age. Early population explosion leads to establishment of first colonies in the Greek islands and Asia Minor.

800–600
The age of Homer's *Odyssey* and the *Iliad*. The first city-states emerge, the functions of kings taken over by annual appointments of 'archons' from the most important families.

776
Probable date of the first Olympic Games.

620
Draco formalises the laws of Athens and Attica, their strictness giving us the word 'Draconian'.

520–430
The Persian Wars.

490
The Battle of Marathon

and the defeat of the invading Persians.

480
The Persians gain their revenge at Thermopylae and take Athens, but the Athenians then win the Battle of Salamis.

479
The Persians are finally defeated.

480–430
The Golden Age of Pericles, the building of the Parthenon, the era of Sophocles, Aeschylus and Euripides.

429
Death of Pericles.

431–404
The Peloponnesian War results in the defeat of Athens by Sparta.

371
Sparta in its turn defeated by Thebes.

338
Philip II of Macedon conquers and rules Greece.

336
The murder of Philip II and the succession of his son, Alexander the Great.

336–323
The age of Alexander the Great. His empire extends throughout the

Middle East, the Mediterranean and as far as India.

323
The death of Alexander the Great.

200 BC–AD 300
The Romans conquer and rule Greece.

AD 324
Emperor Constantine establishes Constantinople (formerly Byzantium and now Istanbul) as the capital of the eastern part of the Roman Empire.

1204
Franks and Venetians take Constantinople and divide Greece between them.

1261–2
Byzantine Empire retakes Constantinople and much of mainland Greece.

1429
The Turks capture Thessaloníki.

1453
Fall of Constantinople and the end of the Byzantine Empire.

1453–1821
Greece is under Turkish rule.

1685–99
The Venetians recapture the Peloponnese.

The Elgin Marbles, displayed in the British Museum

1821–9
The Greek War of Independence.

1832
Prince Otto of Bavaria elected the first king of the modern Greek state.

1881
Thessalía (Thessaly) recovered by Greece from the Turks.

1912
First Balkan War in which Greece regains Thessaloníki and Ípeiros (Epirus) from the Turks.

1913
Second Balkan War in which Greece joins Serbia against Bulgaria.

1917
Greece enters World War I on the side of the Allies.

1920–3
Greece continues a misjudged war against Turkey, ending in defeat.

1923
The exchange of populations: 1 million Greeks in Turkey return to their homeland while 400,000 Muslims leave Greece for Turkey.

1940
Mussolini demands access to Greek ports in World War II, to which the Greek General Metaxas gives a one-word answer: 'No'.

1941
The Italian and German invasions.

1944
Greece is liberated.

1944–9
Greece continues in turmoil as a civil war rages between communist and right-wing government forces.

1951
Greece joins NATO.

1952
Greek women receive the vote.

1967
A military junta seizes power compelling King Constantine to flee into exile. Rule of the Colonels, under Colonel Papadopoulos.

1974
The junta is overthrown and democracy returned, but at a price: the collapse of the junta was primarily due to the Turkish invasion of the northern part of Cyprus.

1975
A new republican constitution means the final abandonment of the monarchy.

1981
Greece joins the European Community.

Peace & Quiet

Anyone who has first visited the tourist resorts in the Greek Islands will be astonished at the contrast with parts of the mainland. It is often forgotten that Greece is a rugged and mountainous country, with many remote places where wildlife flourishes and the more adventurous traveller can find solitude. Some of these areas are among Greece's greatest attractions, for those prepared to seek them out.

Límni Préspa (The Prespa Lakes)

A national park was established in the Préspa region in 1974, with the aim of protecting its rare and threatened bird species. The two Préspa lakes (► 22) which lie partly within the park boundaries mean that this is the only Greek national park whose main element is water. The area is sparsely populated, with only a handful of unspoilt villages,

and the visitor will find rare attractions that are sure to reward a visit. Birdwatchers can look for the Dalmatian pelicans: with a world population of less than 1,000 pairs, one-sixth nests at Préspa. The goosander and the great white egret are also found here, while raptors include the golden eagle, booted eagle, short-toed eagle and peregrine falcon. Mammals are rarely seen, although there are brown bears, wolves, wild cats and badgers.

The Évros Delta

The Évros river flows into Greece from Bulgaria, and for much of its length forms the

Above: *peace and solitude whilst fishing for frogs on Lake Pamvótis in Ípeiros*

Greek boundary with Turkey. Its delta is one of the most important wetlands in the Balkans, and until recently a permit was needed in order to visit the area. It is a vital breeding and wintering ground for many migrating birds, with over 300 species observed here, out of the 400 or so found in Greece. As many as 100,000 wildfowl winter here. Sea eagles and osprey can be found, alongside swans, egrets, cormorants, geese, pelicans, cranes, ibis and spoonbills. Évros is also the only nesting place in Europe for the spur-winged plover. Many amphibians and reptiles, including poisonous snakes, live alongside mammals such as otters, polecats, jackals and wolves.

The Dadia Forest

In the region of eastern Thráki that thrusts up between Turkey and Bulgaria is a series of wooded hills known as the Dadia Forest. They are mainly a mix of Calabrian and black pine trees, and are one of the best places in Europe for seeing birds of prey. Of the 39 European species, 26 live and nest permanently in the Dadia Forest. It is one of the last strongholds in eastern Europe for the black vulture, with about 20–30 individuals, and Greece's rarest bird of prey, the sea eagle, also nests in the forest. There is an observatory for watching the birds, and an information centre and small guesthouse.

Below: *the road to Mikró Pápingo in Zagória, a habitat for eagles*

The Sea Eagle

The white-tailed or grey eagle, found in Greece and other parts of Europe, is one of eight species of sea eagle with habitats around the world. Despite the name they are not purely fish eaters and will eat carrion as well as catching larger birds and mammals.
They can grow up to almost a metre in length and have a wingspan of about 2m.

13

Famous of Mainland Greece

Alexander the Great

Alexander (356–323 BC) was the son of King Philip II of Macedon, and both were born in Pélla in modern Makedonía (Macedonia). During the reigns of Philip and

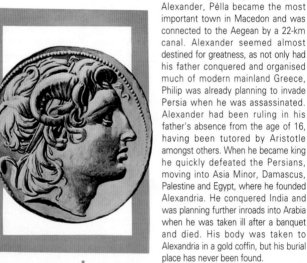

Alexander, Pélla became the most important town in Macedon and was connected to the Aegean by a 22-km canal. Alexander seemed almost destined for greatness, as not only had his father conquered and organised much of modern mainland Greece, Philip was already planning to invade Persia when he was assassinated. Alexander had been ruling in his father's absence from the age of 16, having been tutored by Aristotle amongst others. When he became king he quickly defeated the Persians, moving into Asia Minor, Damascus, Palestine and Egypt, where he founded Alexandria. He conquered India and was planning further inroads into Arabia when he was taken ill after a banquet and died. His body was taken to Alexandria in a gold coffin, but his burial place has never been found.

Coin depicting Alexander the Great, with ram's horns signifying his divinity

Greek Drama
Alongside the development of philosophy in ancient Athens came a flourishing of culture, especially drama. Aeschylus (525–456 BC) was the founder of European drama and the first to introduce a second character, allowing for dialogue. Sophocles (c496–406 BC) added a third character and reduced the rôle of the Greek chorus, while Euripides (c485–c406 BC) went further and created more psychological drama by showing that man, not the gods, was master of his own fate. Among his plays were *Medea*, *Electra* and the *Trojan Women*.

Socrates

Socrates (469–399 BC) was born in Athens and lived his entire life there. He wrote no books, had no formal school or set of followers, yet he became one of the greatest figures in early philosophy, alongside Plato and Aristotle. Greek philosophy is either pre-Socratic or post-Socratic, yet Socrates himself was an unprepossessing figure, being apparently both fat and rather ugly. Much of what we know about him comes through the eyes of others who lived in that same golden era, such as Aristophanes, Xenophon and Plato. Plato studied under Socrates and it was he who recorded some of the famous Socratic dialogues in which the philosopher explored concepts such as courage and justice in an attempt to understand what they meant. What might seem enlightened today was seen as threatening at the time, and Socrates was accused of corrupting the youth of Athens and of a lack of respect. He was tried at the age of 70, turned down the option of paying a fine, rejected the opportunity of escaping from prison, and was condemned to die by drinking hemlock.

Top Ten

1
Ágio Óros (Mount Áthos)

📍 29C3

🚌 Thessaloníki

🚢 From Ouranópoli

✋ Boat trip: moderate

↔️ Thessaloníki (➤ 64),
Chalkidikí (➤ 70)

❓ Tour boats leave daily in
season from Ouranópoli,
also from Órmos
Panagías on Sithonía in
Chalkidikí. Others from
the island of Thásos sail
down the eastern coast
of Áthos. Trips last 4–6
hours and the trip is open
to both men and women

*Known to Greeks as the Holy Mountain,
Áthos has an atmosphere to it that is unique in
Greece, perhaps in the world.*

The first community of monks on the promontory – the
easternmost of the three-pronged Chalkidikí peninsula –
goes back to 963 when St Athanasius founded the Great
Lavra monastery, though Áthos was already considered
a holy site which attracted many hermits. Other monasteries followed in the 10th and 11th centuries, until at one
time there were said to be 40 monasteries with 1,000
monks in each.

No woman has been allowed access since AD 1060,
when Emperor Constantine Monomachos of Byzantium
issued an edict banning all females from visiting Áthos,
which was reserved for the presence of the Virgin Mary.

In 1926 the Greek government passed a legislative
decree which made Áthos a Theocratic Republic, giving it
autonomy but within the Greek state. The numbers of
monks declined in the 20th century, down to
about 1,000 at one point, but a recent revival of
interest in religion, and the monastic life, means
there are now about 1,700 monks divided
among the 20 or so inhabited monasteries.

*Mist surrounds Mount
Áthos with (inset) its
dramatic monasteries*

To visit Mount Áthos – which in addition to the fasci-
nation of its holy lifestyle is a wonderfully wooded and
unspoilt region – male visitors must apply, through their
consul, for a permit from either the Ministry of Foreign
Affairs in Athens or the Ministry of Macedonia and Thrace
in Thessaloníki.

2
Akrópoli (The Acropolis)

The Acropolis, crowned by the Parthenón, dominates central Athens and is a constant reminder of the city's past.

 34C2

🚇 Monastiráki or Thiseío

The word *akrópoli* means 'upper city', and it was on the southern slopes of the Acropolis, in about 3000 BC, that the first evidence of man's presence in Athens was found. Today it is the focus of tourists and is easily the single most important sight to see in mainland Greece, so much so that the main buildings, including the Parthenón, have been roped off to prevent them from being trampled away under too many feet.

The Parthenón is the centrepoint of the rocky Acropolis, and rightly so. It is one of the world's most beautiful buildings, erected during the 5th century BC when Pericles ruled during a golden period of Athenian development. The main sculptor was Pheidias, generally regarded as one of the best that Greece has ever seen.

Several other buildings make up the Acropolis, including the Propýlaia, which was the original imposing gateway, the small Naós Apteroú Níkis (Temple of Athena Nike), and the Eréchtheion. A fascinating collection of statues, masks, friezes and other finds are on display in the **Mouseío Akropóleos** (Acropolis Museum), though the grander Kéntro Meletón Akropóleos (Acropolis Study Centre, ➤ 32) is being built to house some of the best of these in more impressive surrounds.

The Acropolis as seen from the Pnýka

❓ Sound and light show, seating and tickets on the Pnýka

Acropolis Site and Museum

☎ Site: 321 0219; Museum: 323 6665

🕐 Site: Mon–Fri 8–7, Sat–Sun 8:30–2:30. Closed public hols; Museum: Mon 10:30–6:30, Tue–Sun 8:30–6:30, Sat–Sun 8–2:30. Closed public hols

✋ Combined ticket for site and museum: expensive. Free to EU citizens on Sun

3
Delfoí (Delphi)

✚ 28B2

☎ Site and museum: 0265 82312

🕐 Site: Mon–Fri 7:30–6:30, Sat–Sun 8:30–3; Museum: Mon 12–6:30, Tue–Fri 7:30–7:30, Sat–Sun 8:30–3

🍴 In nearby village of Delfoí (££)

♿ None

✋ Expensive; free to EU citizens on Sun

↔ Aráchova (► 52), Ósios Loúkas (► 55)

❓ Guided tours available in several languages

The Sacred Way passes the Athenian Treasury (main picture) with the theatre at Delphi (inset)

The Ancient Greeks believed Delphi to be the centre of the world, and anyone visiting this most beautiful of Classical Greek sites today will understand why.

Delphi has an indisputable atmosphere, which cannot easily be put into words, and an impressive setting against a backdrop of cliffs, with views across a valley filled with olive trees which sweeps down towards the coast.

Pilgrims visited the oracles at Delphi in vast numbers, from roughly the 12th century BC to the 4th century AD. They came on the seventh day of each month, to seek guidance in matters large and small. The most famous of all the oracles was the Sibyl, whose rock can still be seen today at the side of the Sacred Way which winds from the entrance up to the remains of the Temple of Apollo. On its way it passes the Treasury of the Athenians, where offerings would be deposited.

The temple ruins date from the 4th century BC, as does the 5,000-seat theatre behind. Climb to the top row of the theatre for one of the best views over the site and across the valley. Above here is a well-preserved stadium, which could seat 7,000 people and whose starting and finishing lines for races are still present.

The visitor should allow at least half a day to look around Delphi, as the gymnasium and the Castalian Spring are a short walk away. There is also a very good museum which has first-rate displays of finds from this rich site, the most striking being the bronze Charioteer. It dates from 478 BC and is both life-size and lifelike, especially in the detail of the face and eyes, which are eerily haunting as if some spirit was trapped inside the sculpture.

4
Epídavros

✚ 28B1

☎ Site and museum: 0753 22009

🕔 Site: daily 8–6; Museum: Mon 12–6, Tue–Sun 7:30–7:30. Closed public hols

🍴 None

♿ None

✋ Expensive: free to EU citizens on Sun

↔ Náfplio (► 80), Mykínes (► 87), Tiryntha (► 88)

❓ Plays are presented as part of the Athens summer Drama Festival, with tickets available in Athens in advance or at Epídavros on the day of performance

The ancient theatre at Epídavros is the finest in Greece, for its setting, its state of preservation and its extraordinary acoustics.

The theatre was built in the 4th century BC but only discovered by archaeologists working on the site at the end of the 19th century. It was finally restored in 1954. It is said that it is possible to hear a pin drop on the stage from the top of the 55 rows of seats, though you are more likely to hear the voices of young visitors testing the acoustics by calling to their friends. With a capacity to seat 14,000, it is still in use for an annual drama festival held in July and August.

Spectators look out over the site of Epídavros, which was dedicated to the healing god Asklepios, the son of Apollo. The site has remains of a guesthouse, bath, gymnasium and sanctuary buildings, although many are obscured by the undergrowth and a little effort or a site map is needed to appreciate the plan.

Drama played a part in the cures prescribed by the medical practitioners who were based here, but a collection of surgical instruments is also on display in the site museum. This contains a good collection of statues from the site, including some of Asklepios, and a partial reconstruction of the Tholos or rotunda.

5

Ethnikó Archaiologikó Mouseío
(National Archaeological Museum)

*This is one of the world's great museums,
ranking alongside the British Museum in London
and the Louvre in Paris.*

*An evening production
at Epídavros (opposite)
and The Little Jockey
(left) from the National
Archaeological Museum*

With the exception of such gems as the 'Elgin Marbles' and the *Venus de Milo*, in those London and Paris museums, this building houses the best and most beautiful of all the magnificent treasures to have been dug from the Greek earth over the centuries. Among the unmissable treasures are the finds from the Mycenaean chamber tombs discovered by Heinrich Schliemann and featuring exquisite golden items, such as the death mask which Schliemann thought bore the face of King Agamemnon. A magnificent silver bull's head with golden horns is also one of the Mycenaean highlights. Two of the most stunning statues elsewhere are an imposing bronze of Poseidon (*c*450 BC) and another bronze showing a boy jockey on a horse (2nd century BC). Both bronzes were found together in the seas off Cape Artemision on the island of Évvoia in 1927.

These are merely a few jewels picked out, not from a crown but a whole treasure chest full of jewels: Cycladic vases, tombstones, friezes, surprisingly sensual statues, muscled warriors, neolithic idols... and real jewellery.

Upstairs is a special exhibition of frescoes found at Thíra (Santoríni) and dating from around 1500 BC. There are wall paintings of monkeys and antelopes, and one of two boys boxing. They have been reconstructed to show what a typical house of the time would have looked like, with these fine, colourful designs in great contrast to the white-washed cubic look of the Greek Islands today. There are also changing temporary exhibitions, and the sheer size of the collection, let alone the time spent admiring the objects, means that at least half a day should be allowed for a visit.

✠ 34C4

✉ 28 Oktovríou (Patisíon) 44

☎ 821 7717/24

🕐 Mon 12:30–7, Tue–Fri 8–7, Sat–Sun 8:30–3. Closed public hols

🍴 Café (££)

Ⓜ Omónoia

♿ None

✋ Expensive; free to EU citizens on Sun

❓ Guided tours available in several languages

6
Límni Préspa (Préspa Lakes)

 28B4

Information Centre

 Ágios Germanós

☎ 0385 51452

🕐 Mar–Sep, daily
9:30–1:30, 5–7:30;
Oct–Feb, daily 10–2

🍴 In Ágios Germanós,
Psarádes and
Mikrolímni (£)

 None

 Kastoriá (► 72)

Hidden away in a magnificently remote and stunningly beautiful part of northwest Greece is the Préspa National Park – a treat to be savoured.

Where the borders of Greece join those of Albania and the Former Yugoslav Republic of Macedonia, lie the two Préspa lakes in an area of outstanding natural beauty. In fact the borders of the three countries meet in the middle of the Megáli Préspa, the Great Préspa lake, while the southern end of the Mikrí Préspa, the Little Préspa lake, lies in Albania.

Regardless of boundaries, the region is magnificent. Snow-capped mountains are reflected in the deep blue waters of the lakes, which are home to rare wildlife (► 12). There is little concession to tourism, to help preserve the area's fauna and flora, so the few scattered villages remain unspoilt. Accommodation is limited, as are eating places – visitors are advised to take lunch supplies with them, if travelling out of season.

Greece's peaceful Préspa Lakes, a haven for visitors and wildlife alike

For a better understanding of the Préspa area, go to the first-class information centre in the village of Ágios Germanós (which also has the only post office and two small guesthouses). The centre has maps, leaflets in several languages, details of the walks and wildlife, and also sells local crafts and produce.

Many of the other villages are fishing hamlets, some half-hidden in the reed beds, and it may be possible to arrange to take a boat out onto the lakes with one of the local fishermen. The smaller lake has an island, Ágios Achílleios, with one of the region's many medieval churches, as well as some monastic ruins and even a few families still living there. If you are fortunate enough to be able to visit, you will be privileged to glimpse the real life of this part of rural Greece, little changed over the centuries.

7
Máni

A region of rugged mountains and isolated villages, the Máni has a unique character that seems to have changed little in the last hundred years.

Lying at the southern tip of the central Peloponnese, the Máni's remoteness has led to its most distinctive architectural feature, the tower house. There are 800 of these still standing, up to 25m high, from isolated examples to clusters of them in Maniot villages. They date back to the 15th century, and the reason for them goes back even further: blood feuds. Families in these lawless regions would conduct feuds that lasted for centuries.

The Máni retains its independent air, and the northernmost region known as the Éxo Máni (Outer Máni) has some attractive beach resorts such as Stoúpa and Kardamýli, backed by the Tävgetos mountain range whose highest point is 2,404m.

As the Távgetos range tapers off, the visitor enters the Mésa Máni (Inner Máni), where the Maniot culture is at its strongest and where the landscape becomes more rocky and arid. Akrotírio Taínaro (Cape Matapan) is a cave which is said to be the entrance to the underworld... although it is far from being the only cave in Greece which is claimed as a gateway to Hades. Easier to locate are the Spiliá Diroú (Diros Caves), south of Inner Máni's main village, Areópoli. These are well signposted and guided boat tours enter the caves regularly throughout the summer months. In addition to caves the Máni has castles and many Byzantine churches.

✚ 28B1

☎ Diros Caves: 0733 52222

🕐 Diros Caves: 8–6 in summer, 8–3 in winter

🚌 Kalamáta

🚢 Gýtheio

↔ Gýtheio (► 84), Mystrás (► 88)

The rugged Máni landscape (main picture) with (inset) the spectacular Diros Caves beneath

8
Metéora

✝ 28B3

☎ 0432 22278 for information

🕐 Megálo Metéoro: daily 9–1, 3:20–6. Closed Tue; Varlaám: daily 9–1, 3:20–6. Closed Fri; Ágios Stéfanos: daily 9–1, 3:20–6. Closed Mon

🍽 None

🚉 Kalampáka

♿ None

✋ Cheap

To witness, for the first time, the precipitous rocks of Metéora soaring above the plain of Thessalía (Thessaly) is an experience both powerful and memorable.

At first the grey-black sculptures appear to be put there by some Greek god who dabbled in pottery, but as you get closer you see that there is something even more striking about them: built into the sides, or on the summits, are clusters of monastic buildings, with no visible means of access as if they too were dropped from heaven.

How the Metéora monasteries were built is still open to speculation: wooden scaffolding, a network of ladders, ropes floated over the tops on kites to gain the first footing, or a combination of these. What is known is that the monasteries date from the 14th century, by which time the rock faces had already been scaled by hermits seeking, and certainly getting, seclusion.

Of the total of 13 monasteries, only six are today open to the public, although not all at the same time in an attempt to keep some sense of peace and privacy for the handful of monks and nuns who still inhabit five of them. For this reason visitors should dress appropriately: wearing shorts or having bare shoulders may result in admission being refused.

The **Megálo Metéoro** or **Metamórphosis** monastery is the highest, oldest and one of the grandest, while at **Varlaám** visitors can see one of the original ascent towers, in which visitors and supplies were hauled up by rope before steps were carved into the rocks. To confirm that the 20th century has now well and truly arrived for these holy places, the monastery at Agía Triáda was used as a location in the James Bond film, *For Your Eyes Only.*

9
Olympía

Olympía attracted athletes and spectators from all over Greece to take part in the Games, held every four years without interruption for over 1,000 years.

✝ 28B1

☎ Site: 0624 22517;
Museum: 0624 22742

🕐 Site: Mon–Fri 8–7,
Sat–Sun 8:30–3;
Museum: Mon 12:30–7,
Tue 8–7, Sat–Sun
8:30–3. Both closed
public hols

🍴 None

🚆 Olympía

♿ None

✋ Expensive

Games were first officially held at Olympía in 776 BC and contests ranged from chariot races to poetry and music, but it is the running track here which is the site's greatest attraction to many of today's visitors. Temples and other buildings may have crumbled, but the simple running track with its starting and finishing lines still intact seems to put us in more direct touch with the Ancient Greeks as people, just like us. Stand in the centre of the stadium, built in the 4th century BC, and it is easy to imagine the 20,000 spectators cheering the contestants on. Their prize was traditionally a branch from a sacred olive tree, but perks from their home towns were certainly also available.

There is much more of interest to the site than just the stadium, however. The remains of the Great Temple of Zeus (5th century BC) show the effects of an earthquake in the 5th century AD which threw its columns to the ground, and at the opposite end of the scale is the studio of the sculptor Pheidias, who worked here on the statue of Zeus for the temple: the same man was the genius behind the work on the Parthenón.

A cup inscribed with the name of Pheidias was found on the site and is displayed in the excellent site museum. Inside there are well-lit displays of some fine statues, as well as bronze heads, helmets and a gallery of items directly connected with the Olympic Games, like a bronze discus and some starting blocks which pre-date the existing stadium. The star attraction is the Hermes of Praxiteles, a glorious marble carving of the messenger of the gods, sculpted by Praxiteles and considered to be one of the finest Classical statues to have survived the centuries.

The natural rock formations at Metéora (left) and the man-made ruins at Olympía (above)

10
Zagória

✚ 28A3

🚌 From Ioánnina to larger villages

⛴ Igoumenítsa

↔ Ioánnina (▶ 48)

❓ Alpine flowers carpet the lower slopes of Gamíla and Smólikas in spring

The Zagorian region of northern Greece, with its 46 villages nestling against the Píndos mountains close to the Albanian border, remains one of the country's greatest attractions.

Much of it was declared a national park in 1975, and wolves and bears are still to be found here though in very small numbers. The population in some of the villages has dwindled too, with some completely deserted, but there are many larger villages which can be used as bases for exploring the area. Mountaineers head for peaks such as Gamíla (2,497m) and Smólikas (2,637m and the second highest mountain in Greece). A challenge to walkers is to go the full length of the Víkos Gorge, a walk of 13km. This is the second longest gorge in Europe, after Crete's more famous – and vastly busier – Samarian Gorge. In Víkos you are likely to have only a few circling eagles for company.

The walkers of old would make their way from village to village using a series of mule tracks, some crossing the area's rivers on stone packhorse bridges: the finest example of which is the three-humped bridge in the village of Kípoi. These were mostly built in the 19th century by travelling workmen, paid by well-to-do families. There were a number of these, though the wealth came not from local trading but through remittances from abroad, sent by the men who emigrated to escape the region's poverty.

View along the sheer-sided Víkos Gorge

What To See

MAINLAND GREECE

MK

Limni Megáli Préspa

Édessa

Flórina

AL

Thessaloníki

Kastoriá · Véroia

M a k e d o n í a

Kozáni · Kateríni

2637m

Grevená · Dío

2917m Ólympos

Zagória · Metéora · Tírnavos

1978m Ossa

Kérkyra

Kalampáka · **Lárisa**

Ioánnina · Trikala

Igoumenítsa · Ípeiros

Karditsa

Árta

T h e s s a l í a

Préveza

Lamía

Lefkáda

Amfilochía · Agrínio

2510m · Amfíkle

Itháki

Náfpaktos · **Delfoí**

Mesolóngi

E l l á

Kefalloniá

Patraïkós Kólpos

Korinthiakós Kólpos

Pátra · Aígio

Kalávryta · 2376m

Zákynthos

Amaliáda · Kórinthos

Pýrgos · **Olympía** · P e l o p ó n n i s o s · Epídavr

Kyparissiakós Kólpos

Trípoli

Kyparissía · Spárti

Anáktora Néstoros · Kalamáta · **Mystrás**

Pýlos · Gýtheio · Monemv

Messiniakós Kólpos

Máni · Lakonikós Kólpos

Akr Taínaro

Kýthira

0 · 50 · 100 · 150 km

A · B

Above: *Peloponnesian hills and plains, near Porto Heli*

The Temple of Apollo at
Ancient Corinth

Ouranópoli, the gateway
to Mount Áthos

Athens & Around

For all its reputation as a noisy, smoggy, traffic-clogged city (and it is all of these), there can be few Mediterranean cities as pleasant to walk around as Athens on a sunny day. The almost ever-present sight of the Parthenón – one of the world's greatest buildings – and of Athens' other prominent hill, Lykavittós, always raises the spirits.

It is also a place for surprises. Few roads are so modern that there is not somewhere an ancient Byzantine church to add a human touch. Many corners of the city conceal other archaic landmarks, such as arches, towers or the foundations of some great building.

Venturing beyond Athens brings its own rewards: the romantically situated temple at Cape Sounion, the stirring battleground that was Marathon and the peaceful monastery at Dáfni can all be reached within a day.

'The Athenians govern the Greeks; I govern the Athenians; you, my wife, govern me; your son governs you.'

THEMISTOCLES
(early 5th Century BC)

Athens

A weekend in Athens is not enough. It has many fine monuments and museums beyond the best-known: the Acropolis and the National Archaeological Museum. There are museums devoted to music, to ceramics, to Cycladic art and to the military – surprisingly enjoyable. There are temples, stadiums, two ancient market-places, several hills and the heart of old Athens: the Pláka. Nor would a week be enough to reveal its every secret, and another week would only start to divulge the delights on its doorstep.

What to See in Athens

AGORÁ ✪✪✪

It is essential to visit the Agorá to get a better understanding of the ancient city of the Athenians. The Parthenón and other temples stand atop the Acropolis, and the market-place stands below. With the modern flea market just beyond, it is not difficult to imagine the buzz of the original market that was once here.

The imagination is aided by the reconstructed Stoá Attálou (Stoa of Attalos), a stylish colonnaded building which contains the site's museum. Until more reconstructions are completed, it remains our main idea of what Classical Greek buildings actually once looked like, although as yet no one has been bold enough to restore the structure to its original bright colours.

The museum features a small collection with some more unusual exhibits, such as a device which enabled Athens' citizens to vote for the city's rulers, a terracotta commode used by a child and shards used to indicate the ostracism of citizens. Elsewhere on the site is the elegant 5th-century BC

Temple of Hephaistos, the best-preserved ancient building in Greece, also known as the Thiseío (Theseum).

The splendid Temple of Hephaistos in the Agorá

- 34B2
- ✉ Adrianoú 24
- ☎ 321 0185
- 🕐 Tue–Sun 8:30–2:45. Closed public hols
- 🍴 None
- Ⓜ Thiseío/Monastiráki
- ♿ None
- 💰 Expensive; free to EU citizens on Sun

AKRÓPOLI (▶ 17, TOP TEN)

ETHNIKÍ PINAKOTHÍKI (NATIONAL GALLERY) ✪

It is difficult to fully assess Athens' main art gallery, as it has been closed for renovation for the last few years and will only reopen as this book is published. It has never had collections to rival those in, say, Paris, London, Rome or Madrid, but its emphasis on Greek art is admirable, from the internationally renowned El Greco, to the primitive art of Theophilos. It also has temporary exhibition space, so art lovers should check local listings for current details.

ETHNIKÓ ARCHAIOLOGIKÓ MOUSEÍO (➤ 21, TOP TEN)

🕂 35F3
✉ Vasileíou Konstantínou 50
☎ 721 1010/721 7643
🕐 Mon, Wed–Sat 9–3, Sun 10–2. Closed public hols
🍴 None
🚌 234
♿ None
✋ Moderate

🕂 35D2
🕐 Daily, sunrise–sunset
🍴 Cafés (£)
🚌 2, 4, 11, 12
♿ None ✋ Free
❓ Construction of the new Athens metro is taking place in part of the gardens

Palm trees provide welcome shade along pathways in the National Gardens

ETHNIKÓS KÍPOS ✪✪ (NATIONAL GARDENS)

This oasis of peace off the noisy Leóforos Amalías was laid out by Queen Amalia, wife of Greece's first monarch, King Otto. The gardens stand adjacent to the Parliament building and provide the main park in this otherwise busy city. There are tree-shaded pathways, small ponds, a children's playground, a couple of quiet, elegant cafés and a general air of rare tranquillity.

KÉNTRO MELETÓN AKROPÓLEOS ✪✪✪ (ACROPOLIS STUDY CENTRE)

This new project is expanding all the time and while the first main structure is finished, further construction work continues. The whole idea was supported by the late Melína Merkoúri, Greek Minister of Culture at the time, with a view to creating an interpretation centre for the Acropolis. It contains replicas of the main friezes from the Parthenón, their scale wonderfully impressive – a visit here should definitely be made after a close inspection of the Acropolis. Other displays explain the site's construction, how it has looked over the years, and the preservation and restoration work that has been undertaken.

🕂 34C1
✉ Makrygiánni 2–4
☎ 923 9381
🕐 Daily 9–2:30. Closed public hols
🍴 None at time of writing
🚌 230
♿ None
✋ Free

🕂 34B3
✉ Ermoú 148
☎ 346 3552
🕐 Tue–Sun 8:30–3. Closed public hols
Ⓜ Thiseío
♿ None
✋ Moderate

KERAMEIKÓS (KERAMEIKÓS CEMETERY) ✪✪

The cemetery of ancient Athens was situated in the potters' quarter – hence the name Kerameikós. Fine examples of the potters' art can be seen in the museum, alongside gravestones, statues and the contents of graves, some of which are as old as the 11th century BC. In the cemetery itself, many tombstones have been replaced and the Street of Tombs, where wealthy Athenians were buried, is perhaps its main attraction.

KERAMIKÍ SYLLOGÍ APO TO MOUSEÍO ELLINÍKÍS LAOGRAFÍAS (CERAMIC COLLECTION OF THE MUSEUM OF GREEK FOLK ART) ✪

This museum is housed in a mosque just off Monastiráki, built in 1759. Sensitively restored, the mosque provides a bright and roomy setting for the collection of ceramics from Greece and Cyprus from the first half of the 20th century. At its core are some largely primitive but bold works by refugee potters from Asia Minor who returned to Greece in the 1920s.

- 🗺 34C2
- ✉ Tzamí Tsistarakis, Areos 1
- ☎ 324 2066
- 🕐 Wed–Mon 9–2:30. Closed public hols
- 🍴 None
- Ⓜ Monastiráki
- ♿ None
- 🖐 Moderate

LYKAVITTÓS (LYKABETTOS HILL) ✪✪

The walk (or funicular) to the top of this 277-m hill is recommended for the views it gives of the Acropolis, across Athens and as far as Pireas. A visit to Lykavittós is especially popular at night, when the Parthenón is illuminated and there may be a *son et lumière* display to watch from a discreet distance. The whitewashed chapel of Ágios Giórgios crowns the hill.

- 🗺 35E4
- 🕐 Funicular: daily 8AM–10PM
- 🍴 Cafés (£££)
- 🚌 023
- ♿ None
- 🖐 Free access

MITRÓPOLI (CATHEDRAL) ✪

Two contrasting churches stand in Mitrópoli Square. Mikrí Mitrópoli (Little Mitropolis) is a 12th-century church dedicated to Ágios Eleftheríos with a haunting cave-like atmosphere. Next to it is Megáli Mitrópoli (Great Mitropolis), Athens' cathedral. Its main exterior feature is a fine entrance, above which is a mosaic of the Annunciation, this being the cathedral's official name: in Greek, *Evangelismós*.

- 🗺 34C2
- ✉ Plateía Mitropóleos
- Ⓜ Monastiráki
- ♿ None
- 🖐 Free

Lykavittós overlooks modern Athens

Early morning on Omonoía Square (left) and the Acropolis lit up at night (opposite)

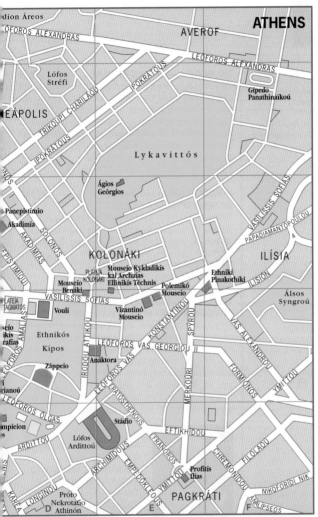

ATHENS

dion Áreos
ÓFOROS ALÉXANDRAS
AVEROF
LEÓFOROS ALÉXANDRAS
Lófos
Stréfi
IPOKRATOUS
Gípedo-
Panathinaïkoú
EÁPOLIS
TRIKOUPI CHARILÁOU
IPOKRATOUS
Lykavittós
Ágios
Geórgios
VASILISSIS SOFIAS
Panepistímio
Akadimía
PAPADIAMANTOPOULOU
SOLONOS
AKADIMÍAS
KOLONÁKI
ILÍSIA
TRIPSISTIMIOU
PLATEÍA
KOLONÁKI
Mouseío Kykladikís
kai Archaías
Ellinikís Téchnis
Ethnikí
Pinakothíki
ILISIÓN
Mouseío
Benáki
Polemikó
Mouseío
Álsos
Syngroú
PLATEÍA
TAGMATOS
VASILISSIS SOFIAS
Voulí
Vizantinó
Mouseío
KONSTANTINOU
SPYROU
VAS ALEXANDROU
seío
ikis
rafias
Ethnikós
Kípos
RODOU ATTIKOU
LEÓFOROS VAS GEORGÍOU II
FORMÍONOS
YMITTOU
Zappeio
Anáktora
LEÓFOROS VAS
ERATOSTHENOUS
MERKOURI
rianoú
LEÓFOROS ÓLGAS
mpíeion
s
ARDITTOU
Stádio
EFTIKHÍDOU
CHREMONÍDOU
FILOLÁOU
Lófos
Ardittoú
ARCHIMÍDOUS
FERRAMÓROS
NIKOFORIDI NIK
KAREA
LONGINOU
Próto
Nekrotafío
Athinón
EMPEDÓKLEOUS
YMITTOU
Profítis
Ilías
ANALIPSEOS
E
PAGKRÁTI
F

MOUSEÍO BENÁKI (BENÁKI MUSEUM) ✪✪

35D2
Vasilíssis Sofías/Koumpári 1
361 1617
Reopens early 1998, details not yet confirmed
Café (££)
023, 234

This museum has been undergoing renovation and extension for some years and is due for completion just after this book is published. The collection of Greek and Egyptian items belonged to an Alexandrian Greek cotton trader, Antoine Emmanuel Benáki. He amassed a splendid selection of artefacts, including paintings, jewellery, ceramics, Lord Byron's writing desk and a complete Egyptian reception room from the 17th century.

MOUSEÍO ELLINÍKIS LAOGRAFÍAS ✪✪✪
(MUSEUM OF GREEK FOLK ART)

35D2
Kydathinaíon 17
322 9031
Tue–Sun 10–2. Closed public hols
None
024, 230
Few ⚙ Moderate

Greece preserves its folk traditions well in museums such as this. On several floors, it contains fine examples of silverwork, embroidery, knitting, weaving, silk-making, traditional costumes, and other arts and crafts. Displays are well labelled in Greek and English, and some craftwork is for sale in the small museum shop.

MOUSEÍO ELLINIKÓN MOUSIKÓN ORGÁNON ✪✪✪
(MUSEUM OF GREEK MUSICAL INSTRUMENTS)

34C2
Diogénous 1–3
325 0198/4119
Tue, Thu–Sun 10–2, Wed 12–6. Closed public hols
None
Monastiráki
None ⚙ Free

This is one of Athens' most modern and most fun museums, housed on three floors in a neo-classical mansion on the edge of the Pláka. It has displays on every kind of music-making associated with Greece, ranging from simple goat bells to the more familiar *bouzoúki*. Not only are the instruments well displayed and explained, headphones at each exhibit allow the visitor to hear them being played.

MOUSEÍO ✪✪✪
KYKLADIKÍS KAI ARCHAÍAS ELLINIKÍS TÉCHNIS
(MUSEUM OF CYCLADIC AND ANCIENT GREEK ART)

35E3
Neofítou Douká 4
722 8321/724 9706
Mon, Wed–Fri 10–4, Sat 10–3. Closed public hols
Café (££)
234
None
⚙ Cheap

This collection of Cycladic art (3000–2000 BC) belonged to the shipping magnate Nikolas P Goulandrís, and is displayed in one of the most tasteful museums in Athens. The simple lines of statues and face masks are highlighted by the subtle lighting, and the influence on modern artists, such as Moore and Modigliani, is clearly evident. An additional wing is housed in a Classical mansion.

Such exquisite Cycladic sculpture inspired many 20th-century artists

OLYMPÍEION ZEUS (TEMPLE OF OLYMPIAN ZEUS) ✪✪

In its day this was the largest temple in Greece, and though only 15 columns remain standing it is still an impressive sight. Work began in the 6th century BC, but it was not completed until about AD 130, by the Emperor Hadrian, whose Arch stands near by. The starkness of the site seems to add to its power – a part of old Athens alongside one of the city's busiest roads.

✚ 35D1
✉ Leóforos Ólgas 1
☎ 922 6330
🕐 Tue–Sun 8:30–3. Closed public hols
🍴 None
🚌 024, 230
♿ None 👐 Moderate

PLÁKA ✪✪✪

This area below the Acropolis may be swamped by hosts of souvenir shops, but it still retains its Greek feel and is just as popular with Greeks as with tourists. Much of it is pedestrianised, and among the shops are numerous cafés and tavernas buzzing with life from late morning to the early hours of the next day. No visitor to Athens should miss it.

✚ 34C2
🍴 Huge choice of cafés and tavernas (£–££)
🚇 Monastiráki

The Greek guards, known as Evzónes

PLATEÍA SYNTÁGMATOS (SÝNTAGMA SQUARE) ✪✪

Greece's main square may lack the elegance of other Western European capitals, especially while the new Metro station is under construction, but it remains at the heart of Athens. Lined by cafés, shops, grand hotels and small kiosks, the sqaure's centrepoint is the Greek Parliament Building (Voulí) where the Changing of the Guard takes place on the hour from Monday to Saturday, and at 11AM on Sunday. It is an impressively precise display.

✚ 35D2
🚇 Metro station undergoing construction
🚌 Almost all central buses

Did you know ?

The Greek flag which flies on the Parliament building on Plateía Syntágmatos was adopted in 1833, but since then has undergone several changes in both design and the shade of blue. Blue and white had been Greece's colours since before the War of Independence, and were fortuitously also the colours of the first king, Otto.

PNÝKA (PNYX)

This wooded hill was the meeting place of the Athenian Democratic Assembly and it was here that Athens' history was decided. There are a number of small pathways leading to the Hill of Filopáppou with its monument to Philopappus, the Dora Stratou Theatre and the alleged cave where Socrates was imprisoned. An observatory stands atop the Hill of Nymphs close by.

🚩 34B2
🍴 Cafés (££)
🚌 230
♿ None

POLEMIKÓ MOUSEÍO (WAR MUSEUM OF GREECE)

The exterior display of Spitfires, Tiger Moths and military tanks is somewhat misleading, as inside the building the museum deals with war in a wider context. It includes some fine friezes and statues, models of fortified Greek cities, such as Náfplio (➤ 80) and Monemvasía (➤ 87), and there are moving displays on World War II and the Greek War of Independence.

🚩 35E2
✉ Leóforos Vasílissis Sofías 24/Rizari 2
☎ 729 0543
🕐 Tue–Fri 9–2, Sat–Sun 9:30–2. Closed public hols
🍴 Café (£) 🚌 234
♿ None 🎟 Free

PÝLI ADRIANOÚ (HADRIAN'S ARCH)

This memorial to the Emperor Hadrian (AD 76–138) once marked the boundary of the city of Athens, where he spent two winters while touring the Roman Empire. It stands at what was the boundary between the old Greek city, around the Acropolis, and the new Roman city, where the Temple of Olympian Zeus is found (➤ 37).

🚩 35D2
✉ Leóforos Amalías
🚌 024, 230

The century-old Olympic Stadium

STÁDIO (OLYMPIC STADIUM)

This gracefully curving stadium, designed by the 19th-century German architect Ernst Ziller, was built in 1895 for the revived Olympic Games, held in 1896. The site is that of the Panathenaic Stadium, where games were held from the 4th century BC onwards. It is still in occasional use, and can seat 60,000 spectators, but the visitor is more likely to see a few joggers pounding the track.

🚩 35E1
✉ Leóforos Ardittoú
🕐 Daily, sunrise–sunset
🍴 None
🚌 2, 4, 11, 12
♿ Few
🎟 Free

The Real Athens

This walk leads from the bustle of the markets, through the crammed junk shops in the Pláka, to the calm of Kerameikós Cemetery.

From Plateía Omonoías, walk south down Athinás. On your right you pass the Dimarcheío (Town Hall), and on your left arrive at the meat and fish markets.

This noisy bazaar shows Athens to be very much an Eastern Mediterranean city and vegetarians may not wish to venture inside.

Continue south towards the Acropolis (► 17), crossing Ermoú into the small but busy Plateía Monastiráki. Leave on the other side to visit the mosque which houses the Ceramic Collection of the Museum of Greek Folk Art (► 33).

Note inside the influence of the potters from Asia Minor. If doing the walk on a Sunday morning, admission to the museum is free for EU citizens.

On leaving the museum turn left and first right along Adrianoú.

This is a good place for junk shops, and buying prints and old postcards. On the left is the entrance to the Agorá (► 31), which should be seen. The temple on the far side of the railway lines is the Thiseío, after which this area is named.

At the end, turn right then left along Ermoú.

This busy stretch of road is packed on Sundays with the stalls of the street market, selling anything from wine and honey to engine parts and holy icons.

If you can make your way through the crowds (movement is often at a standstill), you reach on your right the Kerameikós Cemetery (► 32).

Enter the cemetery with its museum for a peaceful break, though the proximity of Ancient and modern Athens is a stimulating reminder of the city's antiquity.

Distance
2km

Time
30 minutes, excluding any stops

Start point
Plateía Omonoías
✚ 34C4
Ⓜ Omónoia

End point
Kerameikós Cemetery
✚ 34B3
Ⓜ Thiseío

Lunch
Sigalas (£)
✉ Plateía Monastiráki 2
☎ 321 3036

The Ceramic Collection of the Museum of Greek Folk Art is housed in this graceful mosque

Food & Drink

While Greece does not have one of the world's great cuisines, its food and drink are often unfairly criticised on the basis of the limited range available in many tourist resorts.

Tzatzíki
The popular Greek dip, *tzatzíki*, goes back to at least the 16th century. That is when French naturalist Pierre Belon observed that Greek and Turkish mule drivers used to carry with them a sour milk called *oxygala*, which was too thick to seep through their cloth bags. They would crush garlic in a wooden mortar and mix it with the *oxygala* before eating it.

Outside the tourist resorts – and usually in them, too, if you know where to eat – a greater variety is available, including traditional hearty peasant dishes, food influenced by the Middle Eastern effect on Greek culture, and chefs attempting to blend traditional Greek cooking with Western European trends.

When to Eat

Greeks tend to eat late, and seldom eat light. Restaurants are usually open from about noon onwards for lunch, and from 7PM onwards for supper, but that is usually to catch the tourist trade, as owners know the Greeks themselves will not be out in force for some time. Many of the day's specials are prepared in the morning or at lunchtime, and a dish such as *moussaká* may be served lukewarm rather than piping hot – but that is the Greek way. If you prefer your food hot, eat an early lunch or order grilled meat or fish that has to be freshly prepared.

What to Drink

The traditional Greek aperitif is *ouzo*, the aniseed-flavoured clear spirit that turns cloudy if diluted with water. Greeks tend to sip *ouzo* straight, with a sip of water afterwards, rather than mix *ouzo* with water.

No shortage of choice, for those who like to sample the local liquor

As a general rule, the Greeks do not drink a lot of wine with a meal, even though the country is renowned for its unique resinated wine, *retsina*, which can be an acquired taste for foreigners. A young couple or a family out for a meal may well have beer and soft drinks, which is one reason Greek wines in the past have never taken the world by storm. More recently, however, encouraged by the demands of visitors, the European market and more sophisticated Greek tastes, its wine-makers have responded with an improvement in quality and some award-winning products. Look for labels with names such as Boutari, Tsantalis, Kourtakis and Domaine Carras, the country's leading producers.

After a meal it is common to drink a Greek brandy, although this is often done in a bar or at a pastry shop rather than in the restaurant. The brand name Metaxa is so dominant that it has become synonymous with the word brandy, and if you like your brandy smooth it is wise to choose the most expensive type, the 7-star Metaxa.

Greek Cheeses

Cheese is an underrated part of the Greek menu, and a plate of feta, unique to Greece, is a popular starter. Deep-fried, when it is known as *saganáki*, it is delicious. Most regions have their local cheeses, and some of the best include *Metsovone* (smoked cheese from Métsovo), *sfela* from the southern Peloponnese (made from sheep or goat's milk and matured in brine for three months) and the delicious pure white *galotyri* soft cheese, from Thessalía and Ípeiros.

Baklavá *(above)* and some of Métsovo's fine cheeses *(below)*

What to See Around Athens

AKROTÍRIO SOÚNIO (CAPE SOUNION) ✪✪✪

A popular evening excursion by bus from Athens is to the magnificently sited Temple of Poseidon, which stands on the headland of Cape Sounion. To see the sun set in the sea beyond this marble building, turning its columns from white to cream to gold and red, is a thrilling experience. The temple itself was built in 444 BC and was most likely designed by the same architect responsible for the Thiseío in the Agorá (➤ 31), to which it bears a resemblance.

49D1
☎ 0292 39363
🕐 Daily 10–6. Closed public hols
🍴 Restaurants near by (£££)
🚌 Soúnio bus, no number, leaves from Mavromatéon terminal
⬤ None 💧 Moderate

DÁFNI (DAPHNI) ✪✪

Some of the finest Byzantine mosaics in the whole of Greece can be found in this 11th-century monastery. The glorious golden mosaic of Christ Pantocrator stares down from the dome of the church, and below this are mosaics of the Annunciation, Nativity, Baptism and Transfiguration. The buildings themselves are also well preserved, on the site of what was once a temple of Apollo. One of Apollo's symbols was the laurel – or *dáfni*, in Greek.

49D1
☎ 581 1558
🕐 Daily 8:30–3. Closed public hols
🍴 None
🚌 A16
⬤ None
💧 Moderate

ELEFSÍNA (ELEUSIS) ✪

The Sacred Way from Athens to Elefsína is scarcely sacred today, with a multi-lane motorway running past dockyards, factories and oil refineries. But in the 5th century BC, this was one of the most religious sites in the ancient world, home to a cult which attracted up to 30,000 followers. Their rituals were so secret that no records remain – only speculation. A degree of speculation will also be needed to imagine the site as it was, for these days only foundations and overgrown pathways remain, though models in the museum help the visitor create the picture.

49D1
✉ Gioga/Iera 1
☎ 554 6019
🕐 Tue–Sun 8:30–3. Closed public hols
🍴 None
🚌 A16
⬤ None 💧 Cheap

Christ Pantocrator, or Ruler of All, at Dáfni

42

Sounion attracts visitors by day and night

KIFISIÁ ⭐

At the northern end of the Athens metro is the suburb of Kifisiá, a world away – and 276m higher – than the port of Pireas at the other end. Expensive houses and tasteful shops mark this out as one of the more desirable parts of Athens, and the visitor will also find the **Goulandrís Natural History Museum** here, with excellent displays on Greece's wildlife and natural attractions.

MARATHÓNAS (MARATHON) ⭐

In 490 BC news of the Greek victory over the Persians at Marathon was relayed to Athens by a soldier who ran the 41km to deliver his message, and then died. The event is commemorated in the name of today's marathon race, and the battle commemorated in the mound under which the 192 Athenians who lost their lives in the fight were buried. The fact that 6,400 Persians are also said to have been killed indicates the scale of the heroic victory. There is a small archaeological museum near to the modern village of Marathónas, and a track from the museum leads to a hill with good views across the Plain of Marathon.

PIREAS (PIRAEUS) ⭐⭐

Athens' port, one of the busiest in the Mediterranean, is seldom appreciated by those who pass through it. After the calm of a visit to the Greek Islands, or as a gateway to them, it has the kind of clamour which reminds you that chaos is a Greek word. It is noisy and polluted and has a puzzling layout – but it does have its attractions. Not least of these is a selection of good seafood restaurants around the Mikrolímano harbour, while its small **Archaeological Museum** has some striking exhibits, including statues rescued from ships wrecked in Pireas harbour.

✚ 49D1
Goulandris Natural History Museum
✉ Levidou 13
☎ 808 6405
⏲ Tue–Thu, Sat–Sun 9–2. Closed public hols
🍴 Café (£) 🚇 Kifisiá
♿ None 💶 Moderate

✚ 49D1
☎ Tomb and Archaeological Museum: 0294 55155
⏲ Both open Tue–Sun 8:30–3. Closed public hols
🍴 None
🚌 Marathónas bus, no number, from Mavromatéon terminal
♿ None
💶 Moderate

✚ 49D1
Archaeological Museum
✉ Chariláou Trikoúpi
☎ 452 1598
⏲ Tue–Sun 8:30–3. Closed public hols
🍴 None
🚇 Pireas
♿ None
💶 Moderate

43

49D1
☎ 0294 232888 for ferry details
🍴 Choice of fish tavernas (££)
🚌 Regular buses from Mavromatéon terminal
⛴ Daily ferries to Évvoia, regular ferries and hydrofoils to Cyclades and northeast Aegean islands

RAFÍNA ✪

There are two main reasons for visiting Rafína, the port on the eastern coast of Attica. One is practical (ferries) and the other pleasurable (food). The small seaside resort is the connecting point for ferries to and from a number of islands in the Dodecanese, Cyclades, the northern Aegean, and the nearby island of Évvoia, which is visible in the distance. The ferries and proximity to Athens (the bus takes 40 minutes) have resulted in a sweep of good seafood restaurants around its fishing harbour.

49D1
☎ 0294 63477
🕐 Mon–Sat 7–6, Sun 8–6. Closed public hols
🍴 None
🚌 Rámnous/Agía Marína bus, no number, from Mavromatéon terminal
♿ None 🏛 Moderate

RÁMNOUS (RHAMNOUS) ✪✪

This is one of the remotest Classical sites that can be accessed from Athens, though awkward to reach unless you have a car. For that reason you may well have the site to yourself, especially out of season. It was sacred to two goddesses, Themis and Nemesis, but very little remains of their two temples, the foundations of which are scattered and overgrown. Set amid groves of vine and olive, nature has largely taken over, and that is part of its charm. It is a place for imagination, peace and a picnic.

49D1
☎ Site and museum: 0299 27020
🕐 Site: Thu–Sun 8:30–3; Museum: Tue–Sun 8:30–3. Both closed public hols
🍴 None
🚌 304 to Artémi then 2-km walk
♿ None 🏛 Moderate

VRAVRÓNA (BRAURON) ✪✪

The ancient site and the museum of Vravróna are about 15 minutes' walk apart, on the edge of the village of the same name. The site was a centre for the cult of Artemis, goddess of fertility, and there are remains of a 5th-century BC temple dedicated to her, on the site of an even earlier building. A reconstructed scale model of the temple stands in the pleasant museum near by, alongside finds from the area which include jewellery, sacred vessels and other offerings dedicated to the temple.

A Drive Through Attica

If flying to Athens and hiring a car, start the trip by heading east through Attica.

Turn right from the terminal onto the main highway towards Akrotírio Soúnio (➤ 42). It quickly becomes a delightful drive along the coast of the Saronic Gulf.

The Temple of Poseidon is unmistakable on its headland, at the southern tip of Attica. There are hotels here for those wanting to break the journey.

Continue north from Soúnio on the main road towards Markópoulo.

Markópoulo is a pleasant place to pause. There are cafés and, in a walled garden, two chapels worth seeing: Agía Paraskeví and Agía Thékla.

In Markópoulo leave the main road to Athens, and take the smaller road towards Pórto Ráfti.

Pórto Ráfti is an attractive beach resort and small port, set in a large bay: a good spot for a meal of fresh fish.

From Pórto Ráfti take the coast road to Vravróna, looking for signs for the site and museum of ancient Vravróna (➤ 44). From Vravróna keep on the coast road into Rafína (➤ 44), another lively port resort. Leave Rafína on the Athens road (54) but turn right onto route 83 towards Néa Mákri and Marathónas (Marathon).

The memorial mound at Marathon (➤ 43) is on the right, after Néa Mákri. Here 9,000 Athenians defeated 25,000 invading Persians, with the 192 Athenian casualties buried beneath the mound.

Continue towards Marathónas but before reaching it look for the right turn to Agía Marína and Rámnous.

The remote site at Rámnous (➤ 44) is at the very end of the road – a world away from Athens and airports.

Distance
130km

Time
3 hours, excluding long breaks

Start point
Any of the Athens airport terminals; add 30 minutes if starting from central Athens
✚ 49D1

End point
Rámnous
✚ 49D1

Lunch
Xanolia Taverna
✉ Vravróna
☎ 0299 71020

Opposite: *isolated Rámnous*

Below: *the bodies of the soldiers killed defending Marathon lie beneath this mound*

Central Greece

Central Greece is a region of extremes. Its countryside ranges from the fertile plains of Thessalía to the wild peaks of the Píndos mountains. West coast beach resorts such as Párga could have been transplanted from the Greek Islands, yet a few miles inland are quiet Zagorian villages and the second-longest gorge in Europe, the Víkos Gorge. There is also Ioánnina, the fascinating historical capital of the Ípeiros region.

Much of central Greece is mountainous, as it includes the Parnassós range as well as the Píndos. In the foothills of Parnassós is the sacred site of Delphi, and if the visitor can only choose one site to see outside Athens, it should be Delphi, in its extraordinary setting. There are other holy places too: the monasteries at Metéora, peering down from their rocky heights, and the Ósios Loúkas monastery, alone at the end of a road near Delphi, with some of the best frescoes in Greece.

'Delphi I should think the Greekest thing of all.'

HENRY BROOKS ADAMS
Letter to Elizabeth Cameron
(1898)

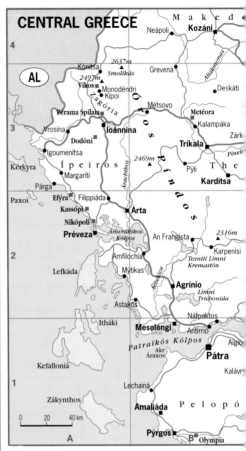

CENTRAL GREECE

Silverwork for sale in a modern workshop in Ioánnina

Ioánnina

The first impression Ioánnina gives, whether you arrive by bus, car or at its regional airport, is that it is a busy, modern Greek town like many others. But Ioánnina is special, a place of great character and a fascinating history. It is famous as the town of Ali Pasha, the murderous tyrant whose presence nevertheless benefitted the area's crafts and culture. It is beautifully located by the side of Lake Pamvótis, with views that stretch across the lake to the southern Píndos mountains, and the lake itself has its own secret: the island of Nisí. The town also has good museums, good local cuisine, and a lively atmosphere.

The small passenger boat travels across Lake Pamvótis to the island of Nisí all day long

Ioánnina was Turkish for almost 500 years, and the results are more in evidence here than elsewhere in Central Greece. There are mosques and minarets, and a back-street bazaar area where metalworkers still practise their craft. Before the Turks the town was Serbian, and long before the Serbs were the Normans, who fortified the town in 1085, though a monastery to St John the Baptist (hence probably the town's name) existed already.

The town's greatest days historically were undoubtedly during Ali Pasha's rule from 1788–1822, when the town flourished as the place of Ali Pasha's court. Many of the Greek residents today prefer to dismiss the period, deliberately keeping his grave outside the Victory Mosque low-key. Ioánnina gained a university in 1965 and in recent years has seen the opening of stylish *ouzéri* and bars.

What to See in Ioánnina

ARCHAIOLOGIKÓ MOUSEÍO   ✪✪
(ARCHAEOLOGICAL MUSEUM)

A reasonable collection, with some interesting exhibits from Dodóni (▶ 52). Of particular note are the tablets of lead showing the kinds of questions asked of the oracle, and two bronze statuettes of children, one throwing a ball, the other holding a dove.

DIMOTIKÓ MOUSEÍO (POPULAR ART MUSEUM)   ✪✪

Housed in the Aslan Pasha Tzami mosque (founded 1619), this is of interest not just for its collection of costumes, weapons, embroidery and jewellery, but for the building itself whose interior is well preserved. It also has exhibits from the town's dwindling Jewish community.

NISÍ   ✪✪✪

The name simply means 'island' and it is one of the town's delights. Boats travel back and forward throughout the day, and in addition to several good fish tavernas, guest-houses, monasteries and the Ali Pasha Museum (▶ 51), there are reed beds, a small fishing community and wildlife such as nightingales, warblers, kestrels and wildfowl. An essential visit.

VIZANTINÓ MOUSEÍO   ✪✪✪
(BYZANTINE MUSEUM)

This small but well-displayed collection of icons, books, wooden carvings and other Byzantine items, labelled in Greek and English, gives a good account of Ioánnina's history. The Silverwork Hall houses the town's best collection, a celebration of Ioánnina's silverworkers, for which it has a long tradition. Mid-19th-century travellers say that there were 34 silver workshops in Ioánnina, when the trade was at its height. There is a replica of a silversmith's workshop with many superb examples of the craft.

✚ 48A3
✉ Plateía 25 Martíou
☎ 0651 33357
◷ Tue–Sun 8:30–3. Closed public hols
🍴 None   **♿** None
👆 Moderate

✚ 48A3
✉ In the citadel
☎ 0651 20515
◷ Mon–Fri 8–3, Sat–Sun 9–3. Closed public hols
🍴 None   **♿** None
👆 Moderate

✚ 48A3
✉ Lake Pamvótis
🍴 Pamvótis (£)
⛴ Hourly 6:30AM–11PM from the waterfront in Ioánnina

✚ 48A3
✉ In the citadel
☎ 0651 25989/39580
◷ Tue–Sun 8:30–3. Closed public hols
🍴 None
♿ Few
👆 Museum and annexe: moderate

Ali Pasha's Ioánnina

This walk takes in many reminders of Ali Pasha's rule, from his walled citadel to the place of his assassination.

Enter the Citadel's main gate on Avéroff, next to a small shrine. Go left down a narrow street.

Soon you reach the old Synagogue (closed to the public), dating from 1790. The Jewish community in Ioánnina goes back to at least the 13th century, but only a few dozen of its citizens survived Hitler's concentration camps.

Continue along this street, which turns right and gives a good view of the Aslan Pasha Mosque, housing the Popular Art Museum (► 50). Head towards this.

The mosque was part of a 17th-century school for Islamic scholars.

On leaving the museum gateway, turn left and keep left inside the citadel walls. You pass a gate with a sign: 'To the Lake'. Go on past this to the entrance to the inner citadel.

In here you can visit the Byzantine Museum and Silverworks Hall (► 50).

Afterwards, return to the gate and walk down to the waterfront, turning left to catch the boat to Nisí.

Boats leave throughout the day 6:30AM–11PM for the 10-minute trip.

On leaving the boat head left for the Monastery of Panteleimon (signposted 'Ali Pasha Museum'), founded in the 16th century.

The museum includes the upstairs room in which, in 1822, Ali Pasha was shot from the room below by his own Turkish masters, impatient with his dictatorial ways.

A walk around Nisí can be taken, from which there are fine views of the citadel. Return to the quay for the boat back to Ioánnina.

Distance
2km

Time
2 hours, including visits and boat trip

Start point
Odós Avéroff, main entrance to citadel

End point
Island of Nisí

Lunch
Pamvótis fish restaurant (£)
✉ Nisí
☎ 0651 81081

Cobbled paths lead to the Popular Art Museum

What to See in Central Greece

ARÁCHOVA ⭐⭐

This is the ideal base for visiting the neighbouring village and site of Delphi, as there are far fewer concessions to tourism. This mountain village retains its Greekness, with a few traditional tavernas, and cafés where the local men gather in the evening to put the world to rights. Aráchova is also a good spot for those wanting to explore the Parnassós mountains, with roads and paths up into them from the edge of the village.

🚩 49C2
✉ 11km east of Delfoí
🍴 Several tavernas (£)
🚌 Several daily form Athens
🔄 Delfoí (► 18–19),
Galaxídi (► 52), Ósios
Loúkas (► 55),
Parnassós (► 58)
❓ Feast of St George,
23 Apr

DELFOÍ (► 18–19, TOP TEN)

DODÓNI (DODONA) ⭐⭐

There have been religious ceremonies on this site since at least 2000 BC, and it certainly pre-dates Delphi. It had its own oracle, and some of the questions put to it are on display in the Archaeological Museum (► 50) in Ioánnina. Dodóni's main feature is its beautiful theatre, built in the late 3rd century BC and one of the largest in Greece. It was reconstructed in the late 19th century, and rivals Epídavros for its setting, looking out across the high valley (at 630m), surrounded by mountains.

🚩 48A3
✉ 22km southwest of
Ioánnina
☎ 0651 82287
🕐 Mon–Fri 8–7, Sat–Sun
8:30–3. Closed public
hols
🍴 None 🚻 None
🔄 Ioánnina (► 48)
👟 Cheap

EFÝRA (NECROMANTEION OF EFÝRA) ⭐

This tiny remote site takes longer to reach than explore, but it is a haunting spot. The ruins are on a small mound, once an island, above what was said to be the mouth of the mythical river Styx, entrance to the underworld. It was the site of the Oracle of the Dead, and the maze of corridors leading into the underground sanctuary can still be seen. Pilgrims would take hallucinogenic drugs before consulting the oracle through the priests of the sanctuary.

🚩 48A2
✉ Near Mesopótamo
village, 22km southeast
of Párga
🕐 Daily 8–5 (8–3 in winter).
Closed public hols
🍴 None
🚻 None
👟 Cheap

GALAXÍDI ⭐⭐

There are several attractive towns and villages on the northern edge of the Gulf of Corinth, and Galaxídi is one of the best. Its white- and pastel-painted houses cluster around a headland dominated by the dome of a huge 19th-century church, dedicated to the patron saint of sailors, Ágios Nikólaos. Along the waterfront are seafood tavernas,

🚩 49C1
✉ 25km southwest of Delfoí
🍴 Choice on waterfront (£)
🚌 Regular buses from Delfoí
🔄 Delfoí (► 18)
❓ Carnival celebrations held
here on a grand scale

and the scene is enhanced by the graceful frontages of 19th-century mansions, once owned by the town's well-to-do ship-owners.

MESOLÓNGI (MISSOLONGHI) ✪

Mesolóngi is known to literature lovers as the place where the British poet, Lord Byron, succumbed to a fever in 1824 while helping the Greeks fight the War of Independence. His statue stands in the town's Garden of Heroes, and beneath it is buried the poet's heart. Close by is the Gate of the Exodus, commemorating a brave escape attempt by 9,000 people, when the town was besieged by the Turks for a whole year. They did escape, but were betrayed and slaughtered. The town itself is otherwise undistinguished, though its lagoons, salt-pans, reed beds, mud-flats, sand bars and dunes attract large numbers of migrating birds.

METÉORA (➤ 24, TOP TEN)

> ### *Did you know ?*
>
> *Visitors to the monasteries at Metéora used to be hauled to the top by rope until well into the 20th century. British travel writer Patrick Leigh Fermor, in his book* Roumeli, *describes his visit to one of the monasteries. About to be pulled up to the top, he asked how often the rope was replaced. 'Every time it breaks', was the reply.*

Some Galaxídi houses are now the second homes of holidaying Athenians

🚩 48B1
✉ 35km west of Antírrio
🚌 Daily buses from Athens
ℹ Tourist Information (☎ 0631 27220)
🔁 Náfpaktos (➤ 55)

In the back streets of Aráchova

➕ 48B3
✉ 90km northwest of
  Tríkala
🚌 Regular services to
  Thessaloníki and Ioánnina
ℹ Tourist Information
  (☎ 0656 41233)

Archontikó Tositsa
✉ Tositsa
🕐 Daily 8:30–1, 4–6; guided
  tours only, every 30 mins
  or according to demand.
  Closed Thu
🍴 None
♿ None
💷 Moderate

Ágios Nikólaos Monastery
🕐 Daily, dawn–7:30PM
🍴 None
♿ None
💷 Free; donation welcomed

*Saint Luke peers down
from above the entrance
gate to Ósios Loúkas*

MÉTSOVO

The mountain town of Métsovo stands near to the highest
road pass in Greece (1,705m), which is sometimes closed
in winter. The town flourishes all year, being a popular ski
destination as well as a summer retreat from the heat.
Despite this attraction to visitors it remains strongly traditional, with a hearty local cuisine, thriving crafts, rich
mansions and a fine mountain setting. It is the unofficial
capital of the nomadic Vlach shepherds, a few of whom
still retain their way of life.

In addition to the delights of Métsovo itself there are
several things to see. Baron Tosítsas was a wealthy Swiss
banker from a Métsovo family who, on his death in 1950,
left his fortune to a foundation to encourage local indus-
tries and crafts, such as agriculture and weaving.

The **Archontikó Tositsa** (Tositsa Mansion), just off the
main street (Tositsa, of course), has been refurbished to
show what life inside such a mansion would have been
like for an affluent family in the 18th century. The town
also has an Art Gallery and a large handicraft shop in the
main square.

In the square are signs to the **monastery of Ágios
Nikólaos**, below the town and worth the 30-minute walk
to see the surrounding landscape and the even more traditional village of Anílio across the valley. The monastery is
tended by its resident caretakers, who show visitors
around the frescoed church, former cells and other
monastery outbuildings.

NÁFPAKTOS ⭐⭐

A well-preserved 15th-century Venetian fortress looks down over the town of Náfpaktos, another of the pleasant small ports along the Gulf of Corinth. There is a good beach and a protected harbour, behind which is the busy main square. The town's medieval name was Lepanto, and it was here in 1571, that the naval Battle of Lepanto, between the Turks and an alliance of Christian fleets, took place. It was the last great sea battle fought by ships with oars, though most of the oarsmen on both sides were Greek galley-slaves.

➕ 48B1
✉ 160kms west of Leivádia
🚌 Daily buses to Delfoí and Pátra
🔁 Mesolóngi (▶ 53)

Náfpaktos fortress once guarded the entrance to the Gulf of Corinth

NIKÓPOLI ⭐

The ruins of Nikópoli are largely overgrown and easily missed from the road, but are worth stopping off to investigate. The high crumbling walls and the theatre are the best aspects. The site was chosen by the Roman Octavian, as his troops camped here before their victory over the fleets of Mark Antony and Cleopatra in the Battle of Actium in 31 BC. Octavian's 'Victory City' unfortunately never prospered, though it survived until 1040 before it was abandoned.

➕ 48A2
🕐 Tue–Sun 8:30–3. Closed public hols
🍴 None
♿ None
💷 Cheap

ÓSIOS LOÚKAS ⭐⭐⭐

In an olive-filled valley surrounded by mountains is the isolated monastery dedicated to a Greek hermit, Saint Luke. He died in 953 and the crypt beneath one of the two joined churches contains his tomb. The churches themselves are among the best surviving Byzantine churches in Greece, and their extensive mosaics and frescoes are renowned. The main church, dedicated to Saint Luke, was built in the 11th century for the pilgrims who flocked to his grave.

➕ 49C1
☎ 0267 22797
🕐 Tue–Sun 8:30–3. Closed public hols
🍴 Snacks (£)
♿ None
💷 Moderate
🔁 Aráchova (▶ 52)

55

In the Know

If you only have a short time to visit Mainland Greece, or would like to get a real flavour of the country, here are some ideas:

10 Ways To Be A Local

Slow down. For the Greeks, relaxing is a way of life.

Use local transport, especially rural buses.

Take a siesta: Greece wakes early and stays up late, but recuperates by closing down from about 2 to 5PM.

Go for a stroll: in the early evening the Greeks do their *volta*, just walking up and down.

Eat late, or you may be eating alone.

Sing or dance, when you're in the mood.

Drink moderately, as although the Greeks know how to enjoy themselves you will seldom see drunken bad behaviour.

Dress appropriately: cover up when visiting churches and monasteries.

Don't compliment Turkey, or call Greek coffee Turkish coffee.

Don't scold children: Greeks have great patience with even the most fractious of children.

10 Good Places To Have Lunch

Sigalas (£) Monastiráki 2, Athens ☎ 321 3036. Bustling taverna in heart of Athens, not for gourmets but as Greek as it gets.

O Plátanos (££) ✉ Diogénous 4, Pláka, Athens ☎ 322 0666. Old Athens favourite maintains high standards and great atmosphere.

Stratis (£) ✉ Níkis 19, Thessaloníki ☎ 031 279353. Popular seafront restaurant, buzzing at the weekend. Simple but good food and quality wines and beers.

Pantheon (£) ✉ In the main square, Makrinítsa ☎ 0421 99143. Panoramic views and regional dishes.

Mikrolímano, in Pireas. Innumerable fish tavernas (£££) around this small harbour in busy Pireas. Excellent but expensive fish. Choose one that suits your taste and budget.

Pamvótis (££) ✉ Nisí island, Ioánnina ☎ 0651 81081. By the boat dock, extremely fresh fish (choose yours from the tank).

Paradosi (£) ✉ Psarádes. Good fresh fish on the shores of the Préspa Lakes.

Lela's (£) ✉ On the seafront at Kardamýli in the Máni ☎ 0721 73541. Lovely sea views, good home-cooked local food.

Kanoni (££) ✉ In Monemvasía old town ☎ 0732 61387. Converted mansion, tastefully done out, good views and good food.

Panos Zafira (£££) ✉ On the harbour at Kavála ☎ 051 227978. Good seafood place, popular with locals in bustle of the harbour.

10 Top Activities

Cycling: increasingly popular despite (or due to?) the mountainous terrain. Information from the Greek Cycling Federation ✉ Vilodrome Olimpique, Av S Louis/Irinis 151, Maroussi, Athens ☎ 682 9140.

Golf: a few courses, including Glifáda near Athens ☎ 894 6820 and the Pórto Carrás resort in Chalkidikí ☎ 0375 71221.

Horse-riding: there are a few clubs near Athens and Thessaloníki, and smaller ones around the country. Contact the Hellenic Riding Club ✉ Maroussi, Athens ☎ 682 6128.

Mountaineering: excellent opportunities, good range of mountain huts and innumerable clubs. Details from the

Hellenic Federation of Mountaineering Clubs ✉ Miloni 5, Athens ☎ 364 5904.

Running: if you want to run a marathon then you may as well cover the original route, from Marathon to Athens. Details from SEGAS ✉ Syngroú 137, Athens ☎ 935 9302.

Sailing: Greece is the home of maritime men, from Odysseus to the modern shipping magnates. Information from the Hellenic Sailing Federation ✉ Fimilinon 7 Athens ☎ 323 3696.

Skiing: Ski centres at Parnassós, Métsovo and the Pílio are among the best, though not to Western European standards. Information from the Hellenic Federation of Skiing Clubs ✉ Agíou Konstantínou 34, Athens ☎ 524 0057.

Swimming: Greek waters have good standards of cleanliness, with popular areas such as Chalkidikí being carefully monitored.

Walking: innumerable excellent mountain walks, not to mention the Víkos Gorge. Go well prepared and take a good map.

Watersports: water-skiing, windsurfing, parascending and other activities are available in almost all resorts.

Freshly caught fish... and food freshly cooked

5
Best Small Museums

- Museum of Greek Musical Instruments, Athens (► 36, 100)
- Folklore Museum, Náfplio (► 81)
- Folk Art Museum, Thessaloníki
- Folklore Museum, Kastoriá (► 72)
- Silverworks Hall, Ioánnina (► 50)

5
Greek Dishes To Try

- *Saganáki*: deep-fried cheese
- *Spedzofai*: spicy stew of sausage, pepper, tomatoes.
- *Gemistá*: stuffed tomatoes and/or peppers.
- *Kalamaris* or *kalamarákia*: fried baby squid.
- *Vriam*: ratatouille-type dish of fresh vegetables.

5
Lively Beach Holiday Resorts

- Párga, Ípeiros (► 58)
- Koróni, Peloponnese
- Ágios Ioánnis, Pílio peninsula
- Stoúpa, Máni
- Kallithéa, Chalkidikí

5
Best Views

- Of Athens: from the top of Lykavittós
- Of Thessaloníki: from the Chain Tower (Dingirli Koulé) in the upper town
- Of Ioánnina: from the far side of Lake Pamvótis
- Of Náfplio: from the Palamídi Fortress
- Of Delphi: from the top row of the site theatre

PÁRGA ✪✪

There are several beach resorts on the Ionian coast, and Párga is the most attractive and most developed. It's a lively little place set around a harbour lined with seafood restaurants. A Venetian castle crowns the headland, beyond which is a long stretch of sandy beach, with other beaches just a short walk away. Despite the numerous souvenir shops, Párga retains its charm and is also a good base for those who may want to combine sunbathing with exploring inland.

PARNASSÓS ✪✪

The highest peak in the Parnassós range is in fact Mount Liákoura, at 2,457m. It is reasonably accessible on foot due to the access roads that have been built to accommodate visiting skiers. Also accessible and worth seeing, though on a narrow, stony road followed by a short walk, is the Corycian Cave. This was sacred to Pan and the scene of orgiastic activity, though if you take a torch today you will only see stalactites and a few inscriptions. Part of the area is a national park, established in 1938 and one of the first in Europe.

PÉRAMA SPÍLAIA (PERAMA CAVES) ✪

A short drive out from Ioánnina (➤ 48) is one of the best show caves in Greece. Remains of cave bears have been found here since the cave was rediscovered by luck during World War II by local people seeking shelter from the bombing. The several kilometres of tunnels have still not been fully explored and it is thought to be the largest cave network in Greece.

Guided tours show the strangely shaped rocks and dripping walls, illuminated by coloured lights. The inevitable names have been given to some of the rocks, such as the 'Sphinx' or 'Statue of Liberty'.

PÍLIO (THE PELION)

✪✪✪

The heavily wooded Pílio peninsula is a justifiably popular spot with Greeks, yet not nearly so well known outside the country. Perhaps the Greeks would prefer to keep its beaches, mountain villages, forests, orchards and distinctive local cuisine for themselves, but anyone who ventures there will surely be enchanted by its scenery and character. Two villages in particular, Makrinítsa and Vyzítsa (traffic is banned from the former) should be on everyone's itinerary, and Milopótamos and Ágios loánnis are two good beach resorts.

✚ 49D3
✉ East and south of Vólos
🍴 Restaurants and tavernas in most towns and villages (£–££)
🚌 Daily from Vólos to most Pílio villages, and to Thessaloníki
🚂 Daily to Thessaloníki and Kalampáka
⛴ Daily ferries from Vólos to all Sporádes islands, and occasional hydrofoils to Skýros
ℹ Vólos Tourist Information (☎ 0421 24915)

The seaside bustle of Párga (opposite), and peace in the Pílio (left)

TÉMPI (VALE OF TEMPE)

✪

Road, rail and river all squeeze through the narrow Vale of Tempe, which is the most convenient gateway between central and northern Greece. The beautifully wooded gorge runs for 10km and was once known as the Wolf's Mouth, which gives a flavour of its dramatic nature, somewhat marred today by the flow of traffic. There are several stopping-off points for drivers, allowing access to the springs and chapels to be found here.

✚ 49C3
✉ 20km northeast of Lárisa
🍴 None in the vale

Did you know?

Apollo washed in the river Piniós which flows through the Vale of Tempe, and fell in love with the nymph, Daphne. She was not equally enamoured and persuaded her father to help her escape Apollo's advances by changing her into a laurel tree. Hence the Greek name for the laurel tree: dáfni.

THERMOPÝLES (THERMOPYLAE)

✪

The Pass of Thermopylae has succumbed to the passage of time in more ways than one. Today the sea has receded and it is no longer the stronghold it was, enabling a few hundred Spartans to resist, for a while at least, several thousand invading Persians in 480 BC. The modern main highway also gives the place a sense of anti-climax, but many people like to stop off nonetheless to see the statue of the Spartan King, Leonidas, and the burial mound of the heroic Spartan army.

✚ 49C2
✉ 14km southeast of Lamía

THÍVA (THEBES) ✪

Thebes, like Sparta, is a Greek name with great historical resonance, which can make the present-day reality of a modern town, twice rebuilt after 19th-century earthquakes, a little disappointing. There are some ancient remains scattered around, and an attractive, if small, **Archaeological Museum**. Amongst its best exhibits are some painted Mycenaean sarcophagi from the 13th century BC. The town's other claims to fame are as the home of Oedipus and the birthplace of the Greek alphabet.

VÓLOS ✪✪

The port of Vólos is the third largest in Greece, after Pireas and Thessaloníki, and not especially attractive as several earthquakes have left a series of modern buildings laid out on long, straight streets. It does have a pleasant waterfront though, and an **Archaeological Museum** set in a large garden is noted for its extensive collections of tombstones and neolithic pottery, unearthed from nearby sites. Vólos is also the port from which Jason set sail with The Argonauts in search of the Golden Fleece. In 1984 British author and sailor Tim Severin re-created Jason's voyage by launching a full-scale model of his ship, the *Argo*, from Vólos. A bronze model of the *Argo* now stands on the waterfront. Today's visitors sail more conventionally to the Sporádes, or drive through on the way to the Pílio peninsula.

ZAGÓRIA (➤ 26, TOP TEN)

+ 49D1
✉ 81km northwest of Athens

Archaeological Museum
✉ Plateía Keramopoúlou
☎ 0262 27913
⊙ Tue–Sun 8:30–3. Closed public hols
¶ None
& None **♨** Cheap

+ 49C3
▣ Daily to Athens, Thessaloníki and villages of the Pílio
▣ Daily to Athens and Thessaloníki
▭ Daily ferries to Sporádes islands
↔ Pílio (➤ 59)

Archaeological Museum
✉ Athanasáki 1
☎ 0421 25285
⊙ Tue–Sun 8:30–3. Closed public hols
▣ 3
¶ None **&** None
♨ Cheap

Into Zagória

This drive passes through some of the most lovely mountain villages in the heart of the Zagorian region, many with magnificent views into the Víkos Gorge.

Head north out of Ioánnina on the airport road heading for Kónitsa on the E90 route.

If time allows, Kónitsa is also worth visiting: an attractive old town with magnificent views of the Píndos mountain peaks which surround it.

After almost 20km take the right turning towards Vítsa, but before reaching it take a detour down a right-hand turning towards Kípoi (Kipi).

Take a break at Kípoi where there are a few of the old packhorse bridges to see, notably a three-humped example at the far end of the village.

Return along the same road, this time taking the right turn on to Vítsa.

Vítsa is a tiny traditional village with tavernas, guesthouse accommodation and access to the Víkos Gorge. Many of the villages are kept busy with custom from climbers and walkers.

Continue through Vítsa towards one of the main Zagorian villages, Monodéndri, but look first for the left-hand turn towards the Oxiá viewpoint into the Víkos Gorge.

The view here is one of the best into the dramatic Víkos Gorge, whose floor is about 1,000m below. A national park was established in 1973 to protect the Víkos region.

Return to the main road and turn left to continue into Monodéndri.

Here there are many well-preserved old houses in the unique Zagorian style, as well as restaurants, inns and churches. There is also a walk to the deserted monastery of Agiá Paraskeví, for another magnificent view of the Víkos Gorge.

Distance
50km

Time
1–2 hrs, depending on length of stops

Start point
Ioánnina
➕ 48A3

End point
Monodéndri
➕ 48A3

Lunch
Monodéndri Pension and Restaurant (£)
☎ 0653 61233

A Zagorian packhorse bridge near Kípoi (above), and the port of Vólos (opposite)

Northern Greece

The name 'Makedonía' (Macedonia) was strongly defended by the Greeks when the former Yugoslav Republic of Macedonia also laid claim to it. Anyone who visits this, Greece's largest prefecture, will be sympathetic to the Greek cause. It has a strong regional identity, no more so than in its capital, Thessaloníki. Europeans were alerted to its attractions while it was European Cultural Capital during 1997, reflecting its rich diversity.

Makedonía ranges from the Píndos mountains in the west, where bears and wolves survive, to Ólympos Óros (Mount Olympus) in the south, the home of the gods, across the Chalkidikí peninsula (the home of the sun-worshippers) and to the fertile plains of Thráki (Thrace) in the east.

Thráki itself has a different feel. While undeniably Greek, it is Greece with a Turkish tinge: mosques and minarets, bazaars and stork-topped buildings, food with an eastern influence.

'Brigands and flatterers, and drunken men who indulge in a revelry of a kind I would rather not mention to you.'

DEMOSTHENES,
describing the Macedonian troops
of King Philip II (*c*349 BC)

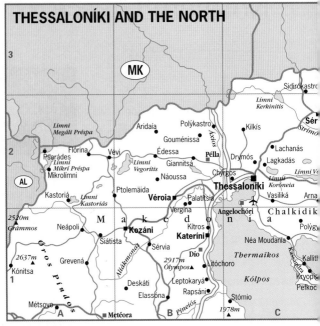

THESSALONÍKI AND THE NORTH

The ancient Arch of Galerius stands in among modern apartment blocks

Thessaloníki

Thessaloníki is the city of Alexander the Great, St Paul's Epistles, the birthplace of Kemal Atatürk and the last resting place of King Philip II of Macedon. It is a city of Roman remains, Byzantine churches, Turkish mosques, film festivals, new museums and old seafood tavernas. It has the buzz of a young city, with a large student population, but the echoes of ancient history too.

It was named after the daughter of King Philip II in 316 BC, the name meaning 'Victory in Thessaly', which was what Philip was experiencing at the time of her birth. By 168 BC it was in the hands of the Romans, many of whose buildings still survive, as does the Via Egnatias, today just Egnatía, which connected it with Rome. Its importance is indicated by the fact that it was made the imperial capital of the eastern half of the Roman Empire, under the Emperor Galerius.

There followed a period of invasions by Franks, Normans, Goths, Slavs, Bulgars, Muslims and others, all

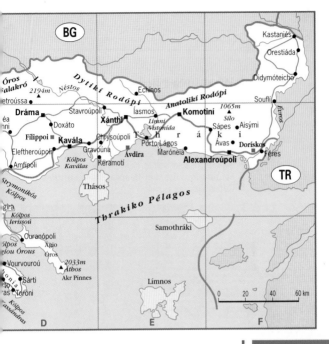

keen to get their hands on this strategic port, the best access to the Mediterranean for the Balkan nations to the north. In 1430 it fell to the Turks, who renamed it Selanik and held on to it for almost 500 years. Their legacy can be seen in the remains of Turkish baths, bazaars and mosques.

Thessaloníki's return to Greece came in 1913, but its multi-cultural nature remains. There is a steady influx of foreign visitors, though more for business than pleasure, as the city's International Trade Fairgrounds host fairs and exhibitions year-round. In summer its airport is even busier, as it is the gateway to the packed beach resorts of the Chalkidikí peninsula.

Thessaloníki lacks beaches but makes up for it with a relaxing waterfront, lined with restaurants, cafés, bars and souvenir shops. It is the place where locals meet for a morning coffee, a pre-dinner drink and for long lunches at the weekend.

Views of the city can best be seen from the Dingirle Koulé (Chain Tower) high up in the old town, where the ramparts are reminders that this was the stronghold, the acropolis or upper city. The ramparts are mainly 14th-century, built on 4th-century Roman foundations. At night the area is increasingly lively, while by day it is a place to stroll and occasionally stop to look down on the teeming city below.

The Rotunda, once linked to the Arch of Galerius by a 100-m colonnaded street

What to See in Thessaloníki

AGÍA SOFÍA ✪

68B2
Plateía Agías Sofías
Daily

First built in the 8th century, this resembles the mosque of the same name in Istanbul. It served as a mosque from 1585 to 1912, when it was reconsecrated as a church; the base of a minaret can be seen in one corner. Although the exterior has been rebuilt over the years, its 9th-and 10th-century mosaics and frescoes have survived fire, earthquakes and air raids.

The frescoed dome of Agía Sofía

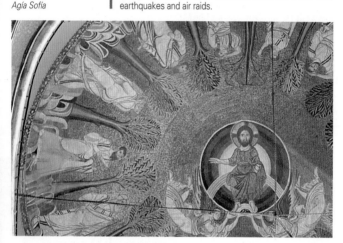

ÁGIOS DIMÍTRIOS ✪✪

68B2
Agíou Dimitríou
Daily
Free

This, the largest church in Greece, is dedicated to the city's patron saint, and the imposing modern building stands on the site where Dimítrios was martyred by the Romans in AD 305. The crypt, place of his martyrdom, reeks of history and should not be missed. The church itself was faithfully rebuilt after it was destroyed in the disastrous fire of 1917, which made 70,000 people homeless. Visit it on 26 October, the feast of Saint Dimítrios, when church and streets around are packed with people enjoying processions and festivities.

APSÍDA TOU GALERÍOU (ARCH OF GALERIUS) ✪

68C1
Off Egnatía

This arch was erected in AD 303 and commemorates the victory of the Emperor Galerius over the Persians in AD 297. It façade is covered in carvings, including scenes from battles against the Persians and other enemies, many naturally featuring the figure of Galerius.

ARCHAIOLOGIKÓ MOUSEÍO (ARCHAEOLOGICAL MUSEUM)

★★★

The star display in this fine collection is in fact a star: the Macedonian Star on the golden funeral casket of King Philip II, found when the royal tombs were discovered in Vergína. The king's skeleton is also to be seen in the special annex which houses the royal finds. Here, too, is the Dervéni Krater, a 1-m-high bronze vase covered in detailed carvings and used for the mixing of wine. It was part of the treasure found when 4th-century BC tombs were discovered at Dervéni, to the north of the city. The museum also features statues, jewellery, glass, sarcophagi and many other items found at several sites in the area.

68C1
Androníkou 6
031 830538
Mon 10:30–5, Tue–Fri 8:30–5, Sat–Sun 8:30–3. Closed public hols
None
None
Expensive

LAOGRAFIKÓ-ETHNOLOGIKÓ MOUSEÍO MAKEDONÍAS (ETHNOLOGICAL MUSEUM OF MACEDONIA)

★★

Greece has some excellent folklore museums, and this is one of the best, in a 19th-century mansion east of the city centre. As well as the usual folk costumes there are carnival costumes, scale models showing rural life in the region, and displays on the nomadic Saraktsan shepherds. Another display depicts the annual fire-walking event held in the village of Lagkadás on 21 May, while upstairs there is a comprehensive archive of photography documenting life in Thessaloníki in the early years of the 20th century.

68B1
Vasílissis Ólgas 68
031 830591
5
At the time of writing the museum was undergoing refurbishment. Opening times, admission charges and facilities should be checked before any visit

LEFKÓS PÝRGOS (WHITE TOWER)

★★

The White Tower was formerly known as the 'Bloody Tower', having been used as a prison and a place of execution. It did form part of the original city walls, matching the Dingirle Koulé higher up in the city, but now stands alone on the sea front, one of the strongest images of the city. Inside is a Byzantine Museum which occupies five floors, covering not just the usual icons but mosaics, jewellery and other historical artefacts. From the top of the tower are good views of the Thessaloníki waterfront. Close by stands a statue of Alexander the Great.

68B1
031 267832
Mon 12:30–5, Tue–Fri 8–5, Sat–Sun 8:30–3. Closed public hols
Café (£)
None
Moderate

The White Tower was built in about AD 1430

🔲 68B1
✉ Proxénou Koromilá 23
☎ 031 229778
🕐 Mon–Fri 9–2, Sun 11–2,
also Wed evening 6–8.
Closed Sat & public hols
🍴 None
♿ None
💲 Free

MOUSEÍO MAKEDONIKOÚ AGÓNA ⭐
(MUSEUM OF THE MACEDONIAN STRUGGLE)

The strength of Greek feeling about Makedonía is shown in this museum, which tells the tale of the historical struggle for the region. Leaflets and brochures are available in several languages, and a great deal of effort has been put into the displays. These include dramatic tableaux in the basement, historical photographs and documents, weaponry, paintings and dioramas. The story of the freedom fighter Pávlos Melás, whose statue stands in a small park opposite Lefkós Pýrgos (White Tower), is just one of the heroic lives celebrated here.

🔲 68B3
✉ Timothéou
🕐 Daily
💲 Free

ÓSIOS DAVID ⭐⭐⭐

There are numerous churches worthy of note in Thessaloníki, but in addition to seeing the largest, Ágios Dimítrios, the visitor should be sure to seek out this, one of the smallest and oldest. It dates from the late 5th century and the tiny chapel contains what is regarded as the finest mosaic in the whole city: *The Vision of Ezekiel*. It is rare not just for its antiquity and beauty, but because, unusually, it depicts a clean-shaven Christ. The church is kept locked but there is usually a caretaker on the site to open the doors for visitors.

THESSALONÍKI

A Walk in the Heart of Thessaloníki

If time is limited, or you want an introduction to Thessaloníki, this walk includes churches, museums and ruins, and explores the very heart of the city.

Begin at the Greek Tourist Office (EOT). Turn right out of the door, and right along Mitropóleos down to the Greek Orthodox Cathedral.

This is not the most distinguished of the city's many churches, but the modern wall paintings and the dome dominated by Christ Pantokrator are worth seeing.

Leaving the main door of the cathedral turn left towards the waterfront. The handsome neo-classical building on the left houses the Museum of the Macedonian Struggle (➤ 68).

An excellent museum with vivid dioramas, old photographs, weapons, costumes and other reminders of the Greek fight for Macedonia.

On leaving the museum take any street down to the waterfront and turn left, strolling by the water to the White Tower (➤ 67).

Now a museum of history and Byzantine art, the tower also has good views of the Thessaloníki waterfront.

From the White Tower entrance cross over the road and turn diagonally left along Pávlou Melá.

There, a small park has a statue of the Macedonian freedom fighter, Pávlos Melás (1870–1904), facing along the street named after him.

Continue along Pávlou Melá as far as the church of Agía Sofía.

Although heavily restored, parts of Agía Sofía date back to the 8th century. It was once the town's cathedral, and served as a mosque during Turkish rule.

Leave the church by the main entrance and walk straight ahead along Ermoú. On reaching the main street of Aristotélou, turn left and walk past the arcaded shops, crossing Tsimiskí to return to the EOT tourist office.

Distance
2.5km

Time
2–3 hours, depending on visits

Start/end point
EOT Office
✚ 68B1
✉ Plateía Aristotélou 8
☎ 031 271888
🕐 Mon–Fri 8–8, Sat 8:30–2
🚌 Bus station on Egnatía, close to EOT office

Lunch
Aristotelous Ouzerie (££)
✉ Aristotélou 8
☎ 031 230762

The entrance to
Agía Sofía

69

What to See in Northern Greece

ÁGIO ÓROS (► 16, TOP TEN)

ALEXANDROÚPOLI (ALEXANDROPOLIS) ⊗

The last major town before the Turkish border is untypical of Thráki, being a seaside resort with fewer eastern influences than inland towns such as Xánthi and Komotiní. It is a pleasant and popular place, with a promenade running alongside the long stretch of beach, which is well equipped with watersports and children's playgrounds. Behind the promenade is an area of packed and narrow back streets, full of shops, workshops, cafés and a few good restaurants. An ideal base for those wanting a relaxed beach holiday, if a little limiting for culture lovers.

CHALKIDIKÍ (HALKIDIKI) ⊗⊗⊗

Chalkidikí has three small peninsulas but four main areas, as visitors often neglect the large northern half, with wooded hills and attractive villages such as Arnaía.

The eastern of the three peninsulas is Mount Áthos (► 16). The central peninsula, Sithónia, is green and hilly if not quite as scenically dramatic as Áthos. It is also much less developed for tourism than its neighbour on the other side, Kassándra. It has its share of good beaches and busy resorts, but a few quieter villages too. The north of Kassándra seems to merge increasingly into the suburbs

✚ 65F2

✉ 45km southeast of Komotiní

🚌 Daily services to Thessaloníki and main towns in between

🚉 Daily services to and from Athens and Thessaloníki

⛴ Daily ferries to Samothráki

ℹ Tourist Information (☎ 0551 228735)

✚ 64C1

✉ Immediately southeast of Thessaloníki

🚌 Daily buses from Thessaloníki

ℹ Tourist information in Thessaloníki (031 271888)

↔ Ágio Óros (► 16), Thessaloníki (► 64)

Kalamitsi Beach (right) and Melion (inset) are typical Chalkidikí beaches of Thessaloníki and is not the place to head for if you want to get away from it all; the resorts are usually full throughout the season, and even outside the main season if the weather is good.

DÍO (DION) ✪✪

Dío was once the sacred city of the Macedonians, and its Classical site and museum are essentials for anyone passing close to Mount Olympus near by. A visit to the museum first, in the village, may help to appreciate the site all the more. There are video shows and leaflets in several languages, and the displays include some beautiful statues which were well preserved when Dío was engulfed in mud after an earthquake.

Part of the site is the Sanctuary of Isis, with copies of the original statues to the Egyptian goddess standing amid the lush greenery. Remains of the town include the extensive bath house, ordinary houses and grander buildings: look out for the magnificent mosaic from a banqueting hall. There are also remnants of a theatre, stadium and other public buildings, all enhanced by the setting between mountains and sea.

🞢 64B1
✉ 115km south of Thessaloníki
☎ Site and museum: 0351 53206
🕐 Site: daily 8–5; museum: Mon 12:30–5, Tue–Fri 8–5, Sat–Sun 8:30–3. Both closed public hols
🍽 None
♿ None
👁 Moderate
↔ Litóchoro (► 74), Ólympos Óros (► 75)

ÉDESSA ✪✪

Greece is not a country of waterfalls, so it is hardly surprising that these at Édessa are a popular tourist attraction. They plunge over a precipice into the Macedonian plain, although the fall is only 25m which, while impressive enough, does not qualify as spectacular. The area around them is appealing, though, with riverside walks, gardens, trees and good viewing platforms. There is also a cave located behind one of the falls.

🞢 64B2
✉ 89km northwest of Thessaloníki
🍽 Cafés/restaurants (££)
♿ None
👁 Free

Falls on the River Voda at Édessa

71

FÍLIPPOI (PHILIPPI) ⭐⭐

- 65D2
- 18km northwest of Kavála
- 051 516470
- Daily 8–5:30. Closed public hols
- None
- None
- Moderate
- Kavála (► 73)

This site to the north of Kavála takes its name from King Philip II, who captured the town from the Thracians in 356 BC and renamed it in his own honour. Most of the remains are from the later Roman period, including a forum and allegedly the prison into which St Paul was thrown when he first set foot in Europe to spread the Gospels. Philippi is perhaps most famous for the battle that took place here in 42 BC, when Mark Antony and Octavian defeated the murderers of Julius Caesar: Brutus and Cassius.

FLÓRINA ⭐⭐

- 64A2
- 35km north of Kastoriá
- Several restaurants and tavernas (£)
- Daily services to Thessaloníki
- Daily services to Thessaloníki
- Límni Préspa (► 22)

This lively mountain town is a good access point for the Préspa Lakes (► 22), 40km west, and it has its own attractions: an old town of Turkish houses and neo-classical mansions on both banks of the river that runs through it. A town built by King Philip II was discovered in the 1930s on the hill where the Xenia Hotel is situated, and excavations have begun again more recently to investigate it further.

KASTORIÁ ⭐⭐⭐

- 64A2
- 210km west of Thessaloníki

Folklore Museum
- Kapetán Lázou
- 0467 28603
- Daily 8:30–6. Closed public hols
- None
- None
- Cheap

This is one of the most attractively situated towns in Greece, on a headland which protrudes into the lake of the same name. Buildings tumble down the slopes, trees line the lake, mountains are visible all around, and there are numerous Byzantine churches hidden away in the maze. Kastoriá owes its wealth to the fur trade and many of the 17th- and 18th-century fur-traders' mansions can still be seen (one is now a **Folklore Museum**). Many of these began as private chapels for the rich merchants, and though usually locked a key-holder can often be found by asking locally.

Kavála

The main town in eastern Makedonía is a combination of busy port, cultural centre and holiday resort. There are some good beaches either side, an Archaeological Museum with some impressive exhibits, easy access to the Classical site at Filíppoi and ferry services to the islands of the northeast Aegean and as far as the Dodecanese. The harbour can be noisy and busy, but there are quieter areas, such as inside the large Byzantine citadel which overlooks it. You are also sure of good food, especially in the many fish tavernas.

ARCHAIOLOGIKÓ MOUSEÍO (ARCHAEOLOGICAL MUSEUM)

The museum has some superb finds from the Classical site at Ávdira, to the east of the city, including a dolphin mosaic and a painted sarcophagus. In fact, a visit here is more rewarding than seeing the site itself. There is also some exquisite jewellery on display, amusing ceramics, vases, well-preserved terracotta, votives, statues, coins and many other fine items.

KÁSTRO (CASTLE)

The labyrinth of streets inside the walled Byzantine citadel (the walls are mainly 10th-and 16th-century) is a marvellous place to wander, with good views and reminders of the almost 500 years of Turkish rule. A statue to Mehmet Ali (1769–1849), who became Pasha of Egypt, stands outside the house in which he was born and which can be visited, though opening hours tend to be rather informal. Mehmet Ali founded the Imaret, or almshouse, on Poulidoú, which was allowed to fall into ruin and has since had a chequered career, most recently as a restaurant. The castle buildings (dungeons, towers and so forth) are also worth seeing.

+ 65D2
⊠ Erithroú Stavroú 17
☎ 051 222335
🕐 Tue–Sun 8:30–3. Closed public hols
🍴 None
♿ None
✋ Moderate

+ 65D2
☎ 051 838602
🕐 Tue–Sun 8:30–3. Closed public hols
🍴 None
♿ None
✋ Free

Opposite: *the splendid mountain setting of Kastoriá*

Did you know ?

The name 'Makedonía' means the 'land of the tall people'. It was settled by a tribe who were taller than average for Greeks, and who were consequently called the Makedni *(tall) or* Makedones *(tall men) in the Doric dialect of the time.*

✚ 65E2
✉ 113km east of Kavála

Museum of Folk Life and History
✉ Ágios Giórgios 13
🕐 Mon–Sat 10–1. Closed Sun & public hols
🍴 None
♿ None
💰 Cheap

Archaeological Museum
✉ Symeonidi 4
☎ 0531 22411
🕐 Daily 8–5. Closed public hols
🍴 None
♿ None
💰 Free

An antique shop in the bazaar area of Komotiní

✚ 64B1
✉ 75km southwest of Thessaloníki
🍴 Wide choice (££)
🚌 Daily buses to Thessaloníki
🚆 Daily trains to Thessaloníki
ℹ Tourist information (☎ 0352 81944)
↔ Dío (➤ 71), Ólympos Óros (➤ 75)

✚ 65E2
✉ 31km southeast of Komotiní
🕐 Open access
🍴 None

KOMOTINÍ

Worth more than a brief visit, this small town bustles with echoes of its Ottoman heritage: bazaars, minarets and a number of people wearing clothing more commonly seen much further east. It also has a commendable **Folklore Museum** in an old mansion, displaying folk costumes and fine examples of local embroidery, and a worthwhile **Archaeological Museum** with exhibits ranging from cave drawings to painted sarcophagi.

LÍMNI PRÉSPA (➤ 22, TOP TEN)

LITÓCHORO (LITOHORO)

Litóchoro is a large village and the main base for those wanting to explore the walks and climbs of the Olympus range, so its streets are often busy with groups or individuals, equipped with the appropriate clothing. This gives it a livelier feel than it might otherwise have, and increases the accommodation and eating options. The area around will also appeal to those who prefer a few casual strolls on the lower slopes of the home of the gods.

MARÓNEIA

Some of Greece's lesser-known sites, such as this one, are all the more appealing for their remoteness and the fact that you will not be sharing them with several coach parties. It is hard to believe that this was once the most important city in the area, as you see the small theatre and the scant remains of a temple and some houses, but its walls were over 10km around in the 4th and 3rd centuries BC. It is said to have been founded by Maron, son of Dionysos, and survived from the 8th century BC until the Genoese period in AD 1400. Ongoing excavations may yet reveal many more of its secrets.

NÉSTOS VALLEY ★★

The Néstos river runs for 130km within Greece, though it begins its journey high in the Rodópi mountains in Bulgaria, emerging at the sea opposite the island of Thásos. It marks the boundary between Makedonía and Thráki, and its delta is one of several important wetland sites in northern Greece. There are many types of tortoise, terrapins, lizards, frogs, salamanders, newts and snakes, though no sign these days of the lions that Aristotle claimed once roamed there. You should, however, see some of the 250 species of bird recorded here, perhaps even the rare sea eagle.

Inland, there is a simple but dramatic drive that follows the course of the Néstos valley and the road that runs between Dráma and Xánthi. This can be cut off in winter, but warning signs will be posted at the side of the road if this is the case. The drive heads into the lower Rodópi mountains, passing through isolated mountain communities and taking in views of snow-capped peaks and thickly wooded valley slopes.

65D3
Northwest of Xánthi
Café in Stravroúpoli (£)
From Xánthi
From Xánthi
Xánthi (➤ 76)
Road may be closed in winter

The Olympian heights can be reached by walkers after careful preparation

ÓLYMPOS ÓROS (MOUNT OLYMPUS) ★★★

Even if only driving by on the main Athens–Thessaloníki highway, the visitor will want to stop and gaze up at Greece's highest mountain, the legendary home of the Greek gods (it was not scaled by man until 1913). The name Olympus generally refers to the whole range, although the highest peak (Mítikas, 2,917m) is also usually called Olympus. Whatever the name, the sight is impressive, rising dramatically out of the plain towards the heavens. Litóchoro (➤ 74) is the main base for those who want to explore further; it is a tough two-day challenge for experienced, fit and well-equipped walkers.

64B1
75km southwest of Thessaloníki
Choice in Litóchoro (££)
Dío (➤ 71), Litóchoro (➤ 74)
To book accommodation in a mountain hut: ☎ 0532 81944; for accommodation at Refuge A: ☎ 0352 81800
May–Oct 6AM–10PM

75

🟦 64B2
✉ 39km west of Thessaloníki
☎ 0382 31160
🕐 Site: Mon–Fri 8–3,
Sat–Sun 8:30–3; museum:
Mon 12:30–3, Tue–Fri
8–3, Sat–Sun 8:30–3.
Closed public hols
🍴 None
♿ None, but fairly accessible
💰 Moderate

Hunting mosaic at Pélla

PÉLLA ⭐⭐

Some of the best mosaics ever discovered in Greece are here at Pélla. The site appears small, and may look – mosaics apart – little different from dozens of others, but this was once the capital of Makedonía. It was also, effectively, the first capital of what is now recognisably Greece, after King Philip II of Macedon defeated the Greeks in 338 BC and brought the disparate city-states together. The large mosaics, depicting hunting scenes, were found in the remains of houses and once decorated the floors and walls of these homes. Some have been left *in situ*, while others are in the museum, protected from the elements due to their rarity and beauty.

🟦 64B2
✉ 11km southeast of Véroia
☎ Site: 0331 92347;
museum: 0331 92394
🕐 Site and museum:
Tue–Sun 8:30–3. Closed
public hols
🍴 None
♿ None
💰 Expensive

VERGÍNA ⭐⭐

Near this nondescript village, the greatest Greek finds of the 20th century were uncovered, rivalling those of Schliemann at Mykínes (▶ 87). In 1977 Professor Manólis Andrónikos discovered a tomb entrance: the tomb of King Philip II of Macedon. Philip's skeleton was intact inside a golden casket, both now on display in Thessaloníki. An excellent new museum leads into this and other tombs, which can be seen behind protective glass. Above them is the Palace of Palatítsia, and near by, the theatre where Philip is believed to have been assassinated.

🟦 65E2
✉ 56km east of Kavála
🚌 Daily to Kavála
🚂 Daily to Thessaloníki and
Alexandroúpoli
❓ Big market held on Sat

XÁNTHI ⭐

When you reach Xánthi you know Turkey cannot be far away, as it has a distinctly eastern feel, especially with its Saturday open-air market drawing everyone from miles around. Xánthi also has some elegant mansions, built for wealthy tobacco barons, and a delightful main square, with fountains and busy cafés.

The Royal Macedonian Tour

A full day's drive, but very rewarding, especially after visiting the Archaeological Museum in Thessaloníki and seeing the treasures discovered in the tombs at Vergína.

Leave Thessaloníki by following the signs for Athens, heading south on the E75. After about 35km turn right onto the road for Véroia.

Véroia is a good place to explore, but its Archaeological Museum is very small and a visit could be omitted if time is limited.

Instead, look for the signs for the Royal Tombs at Vergína, about a 20-minute drive to the east.

Vergína is the place to stretch the legs, and explore the various tombs, museum and palace remains. This is now known to be the ancient Macedonian capital, previously thought to be located at Édessa.

Return to Véroia and drive through, picking up the road to the north, towards Náoussa and Édessa.

The road goes through a pleasant agricultural region, past peach trees and vineyards: the famous Greek wine-makers, Boutari, are based in Náoussa.

This smaller road joins the E86. Turn left for a zig-zag, uphill climb to view the waterfalls at Édessa, and perhaps have a pleasant lunch there. Later, return to pass this junction and keep on the E86 towards Thessaloníki.

Stop at the Classical site of Pélla, at a crossroads between the hamlet of Néa Pélla but before the village of Pélla itself. Although the wonderful mosaics are the highlight, allow time to explore the site where the remains of houses and public buildings from King Philip II's former capital can clearly be made out.

Resume the journey along the E86, all the way back into Thessaloníki.

Distance
240km

Time
4–5 hours without stops;
7–8 hours with stops

Start/end point
Thessaloníki
➕ 64C2

Lunch
Cafés and restaurants (£–££) in Édessa, near the waterfalls

The Peloponnese

The peninsula which most people recognise as the archetypal shape of mainland Greece, with its three smaller 'fingers', or peninsulas, jutting down into the Mediterranean Sea, is also an archetype for Greece itself.

It is an island yet not an island, cut off from the rest of the country by the dramatic Corinth canal. Its history spans some 5,000 years and it has some of the most evocative of Ancient Greek sites, such as Epídavros, Olympía, Mycenae, Tiryns, Sparta and the awesome yet little-known Mystrás. It has important modern history too, in the country's capital before Athens, Náfplio.

In contrast to Náfplio's cosmopolitan sophistication, the Peloponnese also includes the Máni peninsula: rugged, remote until recently, scene of bitter family feuds and capable of weaving its magic spell even over visitors for whom Greece is familiar territory.

'I have gazed
upon the face of
Agamemnon.'

HEINRICH SCHLIEMANN,
archaeologist at Mycenae
(1876)

Náfplio

Náfplio is far from being the largest place in the Peloponnese, but it is certainly one of the most attractive. Indeed, many Greeks regard it as the prettiest town in the whole of Greece.

There are several reasons for Náfplio's charm. It looks like a Greek island port, clustered at the base of a headland dominated by not one but two fortresses. Its streets are old and narrow, with Italianate balconies which are flower-filled in summer. It has a hugely attractive large, open, traffic-free main square, while across its harbour can be seen the mountain peaks of the rest of the Peloponnese.

Náfplio is very cosmopolitan for a small town: it has a range of good eating places, a small beach, easy access to important ancient sites such as Mycenae, Tiryns and Epídavros. It also has a unique place in Greece's modern history, for it was Náfplio, not Athens, which was the first capital of modern Greece. The country's first president, Kapodístrias, lived and was assassinated here.

The pretty town of Náfplio nestles at the foot of the Palamídi fortress

Little wonder that Náfplio attracts artists and craftsmen and is such a popular spot for Athenians who want a holiday or simply a short break from the city.

What to See in Náfplio

ARCHAIOLOGIKÓ MOUSEÍO (ARCHAEOLOGICAL MUSEUM)

Occupying two floors of a handsome and solid 18th-century Venetian warehouse, highlights include many finds from Tiryns and Mycenae, a marvellously preserved complete suit of ancient Mycenaean armour and examples of pottery from neolithic to Classical times.

➕ 83B2
✉ Plateía Syntágmatos
☎ 0752 27502
🕐 Tue–Sun 8:30–3. Closed public hols
🍴 None   ♿ None
💶 Moderate

ÍTS KALÉ

This Turkish name means 'Inner Castle' though it is also referred to as Akronáfplia, indicating that this was the site of the town's original acropolis. Several castles have subsequently existed on the site and all still show some patchy remains. An enjoyable place for a short stroll, although it is more notable today for being the site of the Xenia Hotel.

➕ 83B2
✉ Old town
🕐 Open access
🍴 None
♿ None

LAOGRAFIKÓ MOUSEÍO (FOLKLORE MUSEUM)

This impressive museum is run by the Peloponnesian Folk Foundation and is one of the best of its kind in Greece. It is closed for renovation until 1999, but no doubt when

➕ 83B2
✉ Vasilissis Alexándrou 1
☎ 0752 28379/27502
❓ Closed until 1999

reopened it will have much improved facilities for seeing its extensive collection of Greek folk costumes, old photographs, rural displays, household artefacts and the shop from which it sells local handicrafts.

PALAMÍDI FORTRESS

Inside this huge 18th-century Venetian citadel there are no less than seven self-contained smaller fortresses. It is well worth the exhausting climb up almost 1,000 steps to get there, though access is also available by road. The extensive views are the main reward for the climb.

➕ 83B2
☎ 0752 28036
🕐 Mon–Fri 8–6:45, Sat–Sun 8:30–2:45. Closed public hols
💶 Moderate

POLEMIKÓ MOUSEÍO (MILITARY MUSEUM)

This has a large collection of evocative and often moving historical photographs, as well as documents, weapons, uniforms and other items from Greece's turbulent past. The War of Independence and harrowing scenes from the World War II are both represented.

➕ 83B2
✉ Leóforos Amalías
☎ 0752 25591
🕐 Tue–Sun, 9–2. Closed public hols
🍴 None
♿ None
💶 Free

Náfplio Highlights

Distance
3km

Time
1 hour without stops;
2–3 hours with stops for visits
and views

Start point
Tourist Office
✉ 25 Martíou 2

End point
Steps to Palamídi Fortress

Refreshment
At the end of the walk the
Stathmos Café (£) in the old
railway station, almost
opposite the tourist office,
is a shady spot for snacks
and drinks

*The 18th-century Palamídi
fortress dominates the
town of Náfplio*

This walk explores the picturesque narrow streets of
Náfplio, taking in fascinating museums and churches along
the way.

> *Leave the Tourist Office and turn left past the
> bus stops and take Odós Plapoúta, the narrow
> street slightly to the right, to Náfplio's main
> church, Ágios Giórgios.*

Dating from the late 16th to early 17th century, here was
held the funeral service for Kapodístrias, modern Greece's
first president.

> *Leaving the church, turn left then first right to
> Ágios Spiridon.*

Opposite this church is an old Turkish fountain and outside
the door the mark of the bullet which killed Kapodístrias
in 1831.

> *Turn left out of the church, then left, first right
> and first left to Amalías.*

To the left is the Military Museum (➤ 81).

> *Follow the street almost opposite, then take the
> first left into Ipsilánti.*

The entrance to the Folklore Museum (➤ 81) is on the right.

> *Continue down Ipsilánti. Take the fourth left
> up to Plateía Syntágmatos.*

The Archaeological Museum (➤ 81) is on the right.

> *Having visited the museum, turn right from the
> exit and right again. Ahead are the mountains
> of the Peloponnese. Follow the road up, past a
> palm tree planted by Kapodístrias to symbolise
> the rebirth of the Greek nation.*

A small square in front has five cannons – the Five Brothers
– remnants of the Venetian defences of lower Náfplio.

> *To the left some steps lead down. Turn left at the
> bottom along a delightful coastal path around the
> headland. It emerges on a road which leads back
> into Náfplio.*

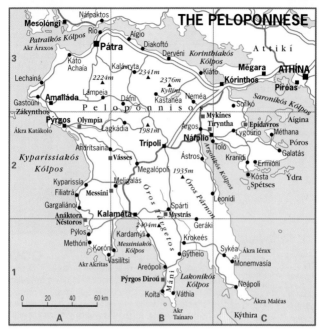

What to See in the Peloponnese

ANÁKTORA NÉSTOROS (NESTOR'S PALACE)

The word 'palace' may raise visitors' hopes too highly, but despite the small and scant remains here, there is much to exercise the imagination. In a beautiful spot overlooking the sea and a valley of olive groves stands the legendary home of King Nestor.

In *The Odyssey* Homer describes how Odysseus's son, Telemachus, came here to seek news of his father. He was bathed by Nestor's daughter, Polycaste, and appropriately enough a bathtub has been unearthed and preserved. The intimate scale of the remains adds rather than detracts from the credibility of the story.

In the nearby village of Chóra, the extensive finds from the site are displayed in the Archaeological Museum, which visitors are advised to see first to help flesh out the bare bones of the site of the Palace.

✦

🗺 83A1
☎ 0763 31437
🕐 Tue–Sun, 8:30–3. Closed public hols
🍴 None
♿ None
 Moderate

Did you know ?

Pelopónnissos *means the 'island of Pelops',*
deriving from mythological times which is strange,
as it only became an island in 1893 thanks to the
Corinth Canal. Pelops was the son of Tantalus, who had
invited the gods to a feast, only to discover that he did not
have enough food. He solved the problem by
enhancing the stew with pieces of Pelops, though Zeus later
revived the boy.

Wooden balconies near the main square in the charming village of Andrítsaina

83A2

⊠ 65km west of Trípoli

🍴 A few on the central square (£)

🚌 Daily to Árgos, Trípoli, Pýrgos and Megalópoli

↔ Vásses (➤ 89)

ANDRÍTSAINA ✪✪✪

There are many attractive villages in these Arcadian mountains, but Andrítsaina is probably the most appealing of all. Once in its heart, the visitor is surrounded by narrow, old streets into which the balconies of the traditional wooden houses jut. It is a place where the long-established basic shops (butcher, baker, cobbler) have not yet given way to modern supermarkets. The peace of the scene is only shattered on a Saturday when the market fills the main streets with the clang of sheep and goat bells and stalls selling locally grown herbs, fruit and vegetables.

83B2

⊠ 12km northwest of Náfplio

↔ Náfplio (➤ 80), Mykínes (➤ 87), Tíryntha (➤ 88)

Archaeological Museum

⊠ Plateía Agíou Pétrou

☎ 0751 68819

🕐 Tue–Sun 8:30–3. Closed public hols

🍴 None ♿ None

🎫 Moderate

ÁRGOS ✪

The ancient acropolis at Árgos is unmistakable, a powerful hill that rises abruptly behind the town and dominates the whole of the surrounding countryside. Those who clamber or drive to the top are rewarded with exceptional views, and a chance to see the remains of a medieval castle which was occupied by the Turks, the Franks and the Venetians, although it is known that the hill (275m high) was well settled by at least the 6th century BC. The town below is modern and not especially appealing, though it has a good **Archaeological Museum** and a ruined theatre that, in its heyday, was bigger than the nearby Epídavros.

EPÍDAVROS (➤ 20, TOP TEN)

83B1

⊠ 48km south of Spárti

🍴 Many restaurants and tavernas (£–£££)

🚌 Daily to Areópoli and Athens

GÝTHEIO (YITHIO) ✪

This small and pleasant port is the capital of the Máni region, but it is at the edge of the Máni rather than the heart. Nevertheless, it is an agreeable place to break a journey, perhaps to sample some of the fresh seafood available at the many waterfront restaurants.

KALÁVRYTA

This mountain town, 756m up in the northern Peloponnese, is where the Greek War of Independence was declared in 1821. It is a place of pilgrimage for Greeks, keen to see the spot where the Archbishop of Pátra first raised the flag in defiance of Turkish rule. Foreign visitors are drawn by the spectacular **Kalávryta Railway**, which climbs for 22.5km from the coastal resort of Diakoftó. It passes through breathtaking scenery, alongside rivers, up steep gradients, through tunnels and mountain gorges.

➕ 83B3
✉ 57km southeast of Pátra

Kalávryta Railway
☎ 01 513 1601 for timetable details
🕓 All year. Several trains daily in each direction
♿ None
🎟 Fare: cheap

KÓRINTHOS (CORINTH) ⭐⭐

The canal at Corinth is one of the wonders of the modern world. It may not detain you for long, but it should not be missed for it is a beautiful and brilliant engineering achievement. It was finally completed in 1893 after a total of 12 years' work.

So too in its day was Acrocorinth, the ancient acropolis whose walls run for 2km along the top of the hill which dominates the surrounding plain.

Down below the site of Ancient Corinth was once the Roman capital of the province of Archaia in Greece, with a population of 300,000, supported by a further 460,000 slaves. The well-preserved remains and the Archaeological Museum on the site help the visitor to visualise the city as it was.

➕ 83C3
✉ 7km southwest of modern Kórinthos
☎ Site and museum: 0741 31207
🕓 Daily 8–7. Closed public hols
🍴 None
♿ None
🎟 Expensive

The Corinth Canal slices through the Greek earth

KORÓNI ⭐⭐

This lovely small resort of whitewashed houses has long been a holiday favourite of the Greeks, but less well known to foreign visitors. It has one of the best beaches in the region, a 2-km mix of sand and rainbow-coloured pebbles. A 13th-century Venetian fortress divides the beach from the town and contains a few inhabited houses and a delightful small convent.

➕ 83B1
✉ 35km southwest of Kalamáta
🍴 Good choice (£–££)
🚌 Daily buses to Kalamáta

MÁNI (► 23, TOP TEN)

Did you know ?

The blood feuds in the Máni had strict rules. Men from enemy families were legitimate targets, but women could pass freely and bring in supplies. Hostilities would cease at harvest times, but otherwise the 'eye for an eye' attitude ensured that, once started, there was no foreseeable end to a feud. Men could remain in their tower houses for decades.

83B2
✉ 34km southwest of Trípoli
🕐 Daily 8:30–3. Closed public hols
🍴 None
♿ None
👜 Free

➕ 83A2
✉ 11km from modern Messíni
🕐 Open access
🍴 None
♿ None

➕ 83A1
✉ 63km southwest of Kalamáta
🍴 Several restaurants and tavernas (£–£££)
🚌 Daily buses to Pýlos
🔄 Anáktoro Néstoros (► 83), Pýlos (► 88)

MEGALÓPOLI (MEGALOPOLIS)

At first glance Megalópoli (the 'Big Town') might seem inappropriately named, but in its day it claimed to have the largest theatre in Ancient Greece. Now in ruins and overgrown, off the Andrítsaina road, it is hard to imagine that this once dwarfed the splendidly restored theatres we see today in, for example, Athens and Epídavros. It could, in fact, seat 20,000 people, and beyond it are more ruins, even more overgrown, and requiring a good imagination to appreciate their one-time splendours.

MESSÍNI

Ancient Messíni is said to have been built in 85 days as this region's new capital, in 369 BC. Today it sprawls over a large area of land near the village of Mavrománti. If you head out of the village on the Meligalás road you will pass through the site's most impressive remains, the Arcadian Gate. This is in fact a double gate, its inner and outer entrances separated by a circular courtyard. Also still surviving are some of the original city's 9km of walls, a small restored theatre, the agora and some temple ruins.

METHÓNI

A companion town to Koróni, across the peninsula, and almost as attractive. Its most striking feature is its enormous Venetian castle, inside which are the remains of houses, baths and even a cathedral – an atmospheric place to wander. The modern town has appealing white-walled houses adorned with bougainvillaea, hibiscus and morning glory flowers.

MONEMVASÍA ✪✪✪

The traveller approaching Monemvasía is treated to striking views of the rock on which the old town stands, known, with justification, as the Gibraltar of Greece. The name means 'single entrance', and that is still the case today. Cars must be left outside the old town: the only way in is a narrow passageway. Inside are some restored hotels, rooms to rent and a few tavernas. With only about 50 permanent residents, it seems at night that you are staying in your own private retreat.

✚ 83C1
✉ 100km southeast of Spárti
🍴 A few tavernas (££)
🚌 Daily buses to Athens
🚢 Several hydrofoils per week in summer to Kýthira and three to Pireas via Argo-Saronic islands

MYKÍNES (MYCENAE) ✪✪

✚ 83B2
☎ 0751 76585
🕐 Daily 8–5. Closed public hols
🍴 None
♿ None
💰 Expensive
↔ Náfplio (➤ 80), Árgos (➤ 84), Tíryntha (➤ 88)

Monemvasía (above) and Mycenae (left) are two Peloponnesian highlights

'I have gazed upon the face of Agamemnon', claimed German archaeologist Heinrich Schliemann to the King of Greece when he unearthed here a golden mask. This and other stunning golden treasures are on display in the National Archaeological Museum in Athens (➤ 21). Agamemnon's palace or not, the ruins here are still among the most popular in Greece, and few visitors will not experience a thrill when passing through the famous Lion Gate. Near by is the Treasury of Atreus, a royal burial tomb that is simple but superbly striking.

Opposite: *a peaceful view of Methóni's castle walls*

87

Old fresco in one of Mystrás' several churches

MYSTRÁS (MISTRA) ✪✪✪

The crumbling and extensive hilltop Byzantine city of Mystrás is one of the most captivating sites on the Greek mainland. Once home to 45,000 people, the only inhabitants now are a few nuns at the Pantanassa Convent, who maintain its church as the finest in Mystrás. Other places to see include the Cathedral of Ágios Dimítrios, with some good, if horrific, frescoes, and the Despot's Palace.

OLYMPÍA (► 25, TOP TEN)

PÝLOS ✪✪

This attractive harbour town is reminiscent of the Greek Islands, with a small port, a 16th-century Byzantine castle, seafood tavernas and an island visible across the large bay of Navarino, site of one of Greece's most famous sea battles in October 1827. The heavily outnumbered Greek ships inflicted an overwhelming defeat on the Turks, which helped secure eventual Greek independence.

SPÁRTI (SPARTA) ✪

Sparta's past and reputation are far greater than its present appeal to the visitor, but it does have some remnants of that illustrious past scattered about the modern town. The hill on which the acropolis stood can be seen, although today it is topped by a church. A theatre and some temple remains are also evident, and the discoveries from these various sites are on display in the town's small but enjoyable Archaeological Museum.

TÍRYNTHA (TIRYNS) ✪✪

When it was established some 3,000 years ago, the fortress of Tiryns stood guard by the sea, which has since retreated. Today the walls of this citadel are over 10m high, about half their original height. They also stood about 10m thick, and Homer described the place as 'well-walled Tiryns'. The walls are still impressive, though the citadel is not particularly high. It was Mycenaean, like Mycenae (► 87) itself to the north, and may even have been Mycenae's port. It is in fact better preserved than its neighbour, but much less visited – an attraction in itself.

✚ 83B2
✉ 6km from Spárti
☎ 0731 93377
🕐 Daily 8:30–3. Closed public hols
🍴 None   ♿ None
👣 Expensive
↔ Spárti (► 88)

✚ 83A1
✉ 51km west of Kalamáta
↔ Anáktora Néstoros (► 83), Koróni (► 85), Methóni (► 86)

Castle
🕐 Daily 8:30–3. Closed Mon
👣 Moderate

✚ 83B2
✉ 60km south of Trípoli
↔ Mystrás (► 87)

Archaeological Museum
✉ Dionysíou-Dafnou
☎ 0731 28575
🕐 Tue–Sun 8:30–3. Closed public hols
🍴 None   ♿ None
👣 Moderate

✚ 83B2
✉ 4km north of Náfplio
☎ 0752 22657
🕐 Daily 8–5. Closed public hols
🍴 None
♿ None
👣 Moderate
↔ Náfplio (► 80), Árgos (► 84), Mykínes (► 87)

TRÍPOLI (TRIPOLIS) ⭐

Trípoli is as near as it is possible to get to the centre of the Peloponnese, and as such stands more as a junction when travelling east–west or north–south. It was a focus of attention during the Greek War of Independence, having been attacked by the Greeks when it was under Turkish rule, and destroyed by the Turks when retreating from the advancing Greek forces. It is therefore a modern town with few attractions, but it does have a number of hotels and tavernas, and an interesting **Archaeological Museum**.

VÁSSES (BASSAE) ⭐⭐

The 5th-century Greek temple in the remote setting of Vásses is one of the most outstanding temples outside of Athens. Indeed, it is thought to have been created by Iktinos, who was also involved in building the Parthenón (➤ 17). Copies of some of Bassae's dramatic friezes can be seen in the War Museum in Athens (➤ 38). The temple stands alone in the hills of the western Peloponnese, not far from the mountain village of Andrítsaina (➤ 84), and is certainly worth making the effort to reach.

✚ 83B2
✉ 180km southwest of Athens

Archaeological Museum
✉ Evangelístrias 8
☎ 071 242148
🕐 Tue–Sun 8:30–3. Closed public hols
🍴 None ♿ None
🎟 Moderate

✚ 83B2
✉ 65km southeast of Olympía
🕐 Open access
🍴 None
♿ None
↔ Andrítsaina (➤ 84)

The sparse remains of the theatre at Sparta

A Drive through the Inner Máni

Distance
130km

Time
6 hours excluding visits;
8 hours with visits

Start/end point
Areópoli
➕ 83B1

Lunch
Marathos Taverna
✉ On the beach at Kokkála

The drive begins in the main town of the Inner Máni, Areópoli, which is more of a village with about 600 inhabitants, tavernas, tower houses and accommodation.

From Areópoli, take the main road south, signposted for the Spília Diroú (Diros Caves). Ignore the left turning to Kótronas but take the right turning clearly signposted for the caves.

The Diros Caves (▶ 23) are one of the area's main tourist attractions, with boats taking visitors into the underground cave network. The trip lasts about 30 minutes.

Return to the main road and turn right, continuing into the Inner Máni. It is the only major road through the region, with few side turnings, so route-finding is not difficult. Any detours simply mean returning back to the main road. One such detour worth taking is a right turning in Álika, to Váthia.

Park in Váthia and take a walk round, as the village has a good number of imposing stone tower houses, some now converted into guesthouse accommodation. There is also a good view south to Akrotírio Taínaro (Cape Matapan), the most southerly point of the Greek mainland, where a Temple to Poseidon, the god of the Sea, once stood.

Return to Álika and turn right on the main road. This is a more dramatic road, travelling up the eastern coast, with superb coastal and mountain views. It passes through several small villages including Kokkála, right on the sea. The road eventually heads left into and across the mountains, and back to Areópoli.

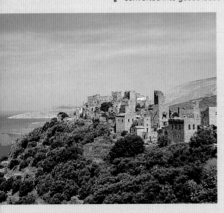

The tower houses in Váthia are characteristic of the Maniot landscape

Where To...

Athens & Around

Prices
Approximate prices for a three-course meal for one person, with a glass of wine:

£ = under 4,000dr
££ = 4,000–7,000dr
£££ = over 7,000dr

Resisting the Touts
There are countless eating places in the Pláka district, many of which aim for a quick turnover in tourists. A simple rule is never let yourself be tempted by any touts trying to persuade you inside. Hardly any of the restaurants listed here need to bother touting for custom, with a regular clientele in addition to the passing tourist trade.

Central Athens

Asomaton (££)
Stylish new restaurant with extensive menu, including vegetarian and unusual dishes such as smoked eel or chicken in yoghurt, mint, mustard and lemon.
✉ Ermoú 137 ☎ 324 6337 ⏰ Daily 10AM–2AM 🚇 Thiseío

Bakalarakia (£)
Simple but good Greek food in basement room in heart of Pláka. Salted cod in garlic a speciality.
✉ Kydathinaíon 41 ☎ 322 5084 ⏰ Daily 7PM–midnight. Closed midsummer

Barba Yannis (£)
Great favourite in student area, usually packed all year round, music, brisk service, limited menu but hearty Greek dishes. You won't find a better atmosphere.
✉ Emmanuel Benáki 94 ☎ 330 0185 ⏰ Mon–Sat 12PM–late, Sun lunch. Closed Aug 🚇 Omónoia

Eden (£)
Hearty vegetarian food blending Greek dishes with slight Middle Eastern influences. Tasty bread, good coffee, non-smoking section.
✉ Lysíou 12 ☎ 324 8858 ⏰ Wed–Mon 12PM–12AM 🚇 Monastiráki

Five Brothers (£)
This friendly family-run taverna has an unusually wide menu, with specials such as octopus or baked aubergine.
✉ Eólou 3 ☎ 325 0088 ⏰ Daily 9:30AM–1:30AM 🚇 Thiseío

GB Corner (£££)
Part of the Grande Bretagne Hotel, smart with piano bar and serving mix of good traditional Greek cuisine with continental cooking.
✉ Grande Bretagne Hotel, Plateia Syntágmatos ☎ 333 0000/331 4555 ⏰ Daily 7AM–1AM 🚇 Sýntagma (when completed)

Gerofinikas (£££)
One contender for the best food in Athens, with a strong Middle Eastern influence. Smart and secluded.
✉ Pindárou 10 ☎ 362 2719 ⏰ Daily 12PM–11:30PM. Closed public hols

Ideal (£££)
Smart and slightly expensive with extensive menu, including 'drunkard's titbits' or prawns with feta.
✉ Panepistimíou 46 ☎ 330 2200 ⏰ Mon–Sat 11–4:30, 8PM–2AM 🚇 Omónoia

Ta Nissia (£££)
Stunning views over the city, matched by the food, especially fresh fish dishes. An expensive treat.
✉ Hilton Hotel, Vasilíssis Sofías 46 ☎ 725 0201 ⏰ Daily 11–4, 7–12 🚌 234

Palia Athina (££)
Old-fashioned restaurant with food, as one local described it, 'from mother's kitchen': octopus in vinegar, grilled feta, pumpkin balls.
✉ Níkis 46 ☎ 331 2975 ⏰ Mon–Sat 12PM–1AM

Palia Taverna (££)
Established late 19th century, and traditional in its dishes and atmosphere. Music, good service, indoor and outdoor seating.
✉ Márkou Mousoúrou 36 ⏰ Daily 7PM–2AM. Closed midsummer 🚌 2, 4, 11, 12

O Platanos (££)

Greek favourite, few concessions to tourism, with tables in summer under the plane tree that gives it its name.

✉ Diogénous 4 ☎ 322 0666
🕐 Mon–Sat 12–4:30, 8–12
Ⓜ Monastiráki

Sigalas (£)

Long-established taverna in bustle of Pláka and flea market areas. Busy, cheap, good range of Greek dishes and good service.

✉ Plateía Monastiráki 2
☎ 321 3036 🕐 Daily
7AM–2AM Ⓜ Monastiráki

Socrates Prison (£)

Unusual dishes such as pork stuffed with vegetables, excellent carafe wine, walnut cake, outdoor and indoor seating.

✉ Mitséon 20 ☎ 922 3434
🕐 Daily 7PM–1AM. Closed Aug
Ⓜ 230

Strofi (£)

Good Greek dishes, especially *mezédes*. Rooftop views of Acropolis.

✉ Rompertou Galli 25 ☎ 921
4130 🕐 Mon–Sat 7PM–2AM
Ⓜ 230

Xinos (££)

In Pláka back street, popular with Athenians, superior food, music late in the evening and lovely outdoor garden seating.

✉ Angelou Geronta 4 ☎ 322
1065 🕐 Mon–Fri 8PM–12.
Closed in winter

To Ypogeio tis Plakas (£)

Great basement place in the Pláka, with old-fashioned murals, good simple food and *retsina* from the barrel.

✉ Kydathinaíon 10 ☎ 322
4304 🕐 Daily 7PM–2AM

Zonar's (£)

Snacks, coffee, delicious pastries, light meals in café popular since 1930s and retaining atmosphere of that era.

✉ Panepistimíou 9 ☎ 323
0572 🕐 Daily 9AM–12:30AM
Ⓜ Sýntagma (when completed)

Zorba's (£)

Typical lively Pláka taverna on narrow street. Lamb Zorba is a house speciality. Amusing décor.

✉ Lysíou 15 ☎ 322 6188
🕐 Dinner & Sun lunch
Ⓜ Thiseío

Around Athens

Kifissiá
Bokaris (££)

Renowned eating place in smart northern suburb, good grilled meat and fish dishes with pleasant outdoor seating.

✉ Sokrátous 17 ☎ 801 2589
🕐 Daily 7PM–late & Sun
lunch. Closed Aug Ⓜ Kifissiá

Pireas
Dourabeis (£££)

Simple restaurant but outstanding and expensive fresh fish dishes from the Aegean islands. One of the best in Pireas, established 50 years ago.

✉ Athína Dilaveri 29 ☎ 412
2092 🕐 Mon–Sat 8:30PM–1AM.
Closed Aug Ⓜ Pireas

Varoulko (£££)

Outstanding elaborate modern Greek/continental cuisine, with unusual menu such as vine leaves stuffed with fish. Booking advised, very expensive.

✉ Deligiorgi 14 ☎ 411 2043
🕐 Mon–Sat 8PM–12AM. Closed
Aug Ⓜ Pireas

Ordering Fish

In addition to the Pireas restaurants that have been recommended here, there are many fish places on the Mikrolímano harbour. The price of fish is usually quoted per kilo, but always ask to choose the specific piece you want. If left to the waiter, you may be served a huge portion resulting in an equally huge bill.

Central Greece

Some Like It Hot

Many Greek dishes are made at lunchtime for serving both then and in the evening. They are often lukewarm, but that is the way the Greeks like them. If you want a hot dish, order something grilled such as fresh fish, *souvláki* or a chop.

Aráchova

Karathanassi (£)

Hearty local dishes served here are cooked simply but well. Strong home-brewed wine and excellent friendly service.

✉ Delfón 56 ☎ 0267 31360
🕐 Daily 5:30–12AM

Sakis (£)

Staple mountain dishes on main village street, including goat stews, pork chops and *souvláki*. Generous salads, lively atmosphere.

✉ Delfón 51 ☎ 0267 31984
🕐 Daily, all day. Closed midsummer

Delfoí (Delphi)

Baxos (£)

Wonderful views down the valley to the sea and good service and food in a village where the large passing tourist trade can result in low standards.

✉ Apollonos 82 ☎ 0265 82448 🕐 Daily 8AM–1AM

Taverna Aráchova (£)

Home-grown food in small and very Greek place. Limited range of dishes, mostly grills and salads, but well done.

✉ Frederíkis 50 ☎ 0265 824542 🕐 Daily 6:30PM–12AM

Ioánnina

Gastra (££)

One of the region's speciality restaurants where meat is cooked in a *gastra*, an iron lid placed over the dish and covered in hot coals or wood. Slow-cooking but mouthwatering when it arrives.

✉ 1.5km beyond airport just before Igoumenítsa turning
☎ 0651 61530 🕐 Tue–Sun 1–5PM, 8PM–1AM

Kafeníon Gynaikón (The Women's Café) (££)

Run by, but not exclusively for, women, this tasteful French-style bar/café serves a wide range of wines, spirits, beers and cocktails, as well as breakfast and day-time snacks such as toast, salads and sandwiches.

✉ Alexiou Diakou 10 ☎ 0651 74678 🕐 Daily, all day

To Kourmanio (£)

Wonderful Greek grill, tiny, always crammed with locals, limited menu but everything well done, generous helpings and service. Try the Flórina peppers.

✉ Plateía Giorgíou 16
☎ 0651 38044 🕐 Daily, all day

To Manteio (£)

Typical non-touristy Greek taverna serving generous helpings including local specialities such as fried peppers or aubergines, various *saganáki* dishes (including deep-fried Roquefort and feta) and *tsoutsoukakia* (slightly sweet, spicy sausages).

✉ Plateía Giorgíou 15
☎ 0651 25452 🕐 Daily, all day

Pamvotis (££)

One of the several fish restaurants on Nisí, this has a lively setting where the boats pull in. Fish fresh from the tank (but probably not fresh from the lake, where stocks have dwindled).

✉ Nisi island ☎ 0651 81081
🕐 Daily, all day

Pharos (££)

Large and smart restaurant on the waterfront with extensive menu including eels, trout, an excellent *gouvétsi* or Flórina fried peppers. Good wine list but some cheaper options too, such as *retsina*. Tasty bread and generous salads.

✉ Mavili 13 ☎ 0651 26506 🕒 Daily, all day

Kalampáka (for Metéora)
Metéora (£)
Simple but good family-run taverna with wife cooking and husband and other relatives serving. Tasty *moussaká*, good choice of grills.

✉ Plateía Dimarchíou ☎ 0432 22316 🕒 Daily, all day. Closed winter

Métsovo
Athinai (£)
One of several restaurants in traditional houses serving regional cooking, with strong game emphasis but several vegetarian options such as leek pie.

✉ Main square ☎ 0656 41332 🕒 Daily, all day

Galaxias (£)
Good examples of mountain dishes including local cheeses and wine, served in delightful traditional building in hotel of same name over-looking the main square. You will need a good appetite.

✉ Main square ☎ 0656 41123 🕒 Daily, 12PM–11PM

Metsovitiko Saloni (£)
Attractive restaurant with mountain décor and mountain dishes, especially game.

✉ Tositsa ☎ 0656 42142 🕒 Daily, lunch and dinner

Párga
Flisvos (£)
Beyond the fortress away from the main waterfront tavernas, with outstanding sunset views, good fish, good prices, good service.

✉ Mavrogenous 10 ☎ 0684 31624 🕒 Daily, all day. Closed winter

Tzimas (£)
The last of several similar waterfront seafood tavernas, and reliably good, with daily specials of freshly caught fish.

✉ Anexartisías 63 ☎ 0684 31251 🕒 Daily, all day. Closed winter

Pílio (The Pelion)
Ostria Taverna (£)
Serves some of the best regional food in the Pelion, such as an established favourite, rabbit stew.

✉ Ágios Ioánnis, one block back from sea front, signposted ☎ 0426 31331 🕒 Every evening & Fri–Mon lunch. Closed winter

Pantheon (£)
Stunning views over Vólos and serving regional specialities such as *spetzofai* (spicy sausage, pepper and tomato stew).

✉ Makrinitsa, main square ☎ 0428 99143 🕒 Daily, all day

Palios Stathmos (£)
Smart new restaurant in village's delightful old railway station. Italian chef serves some pasta dishes but Greek favourites, too.

✉ Miliés ☎ 0423 86425 🕒 Tue–Sun, all day. Closed Nov

Zagória
Monodéndri Pension and Restaurant (£)
No surprises on menu (grills, *moussaká*, salads) but a pleasant place to eat, catering to walkers and climbers exploring the region.

☎ 0653 61233 🕒 Daily, all day

Katerina's Art (£)
Impressive new restaurant in old village mansion with some unusual Zagorian dishes, especially game.

✉ Néa Víkos Gorge ☎ 0653 61233 🕒 Daily, all day

The Service
The Greek way is to serve dishes as and when they are ready, once you have ordered them. If you prefer to start with your starter and then to have a pause before your main course, you will need to order one course at a time or tell the waiter when you want each dish to arrive. Otherwise you may get starter, salad and potatoes all served immediately, and the meat or fish on its own later.

Northern Greece

Greek Wine

Greek wine has never had an international reputation, as most Greeks are happy with the resinated flavour of *retsina*, and many prefer beer or soft drinks. However, in recent years the standard has improved considerably thanks to tourism and increased demand for quality by affluent Greeks. Makedonía is one of the main wine-growing regions, and the Boutari vineyard has long had one of the better reputations.

Alexandroúpoli
Klimataria (£)

On a busy square with a flurry of eating places this is one of the best for fish, but it also has an extensive menu of traditional Greek dishes and some more unusual, such as baked goat. Good choice of local wines, too.
✉ Polytechníou 18 ☎ 0551 26288 ⏱ Daily, lunch and dinner

Chalkidikí
Kostis (££)

One of the more imaginative restaurants in this mass-tourism area, keeping it popular with locals. Care is shown in the way they make their own aubergine salad, by char-grilling the vegetables first. Fresh fish is always on the menu, with battered cod in garlic sauce a speciality of the house.
✉ Néa Fókaia ☎ 0374 81379 ⏱ Daily, lunch and dinner

Ta Pefka (£)

Lovely hilltop setting in pines and surprisingly good food given the reasonable prices. Seafood is popular, such as fresh sardines, octopus *mezédes* or catch of the day, and more unusual dishes such as mussels in a red sauce or *saganáki* (deep-fried cheese).
✉ Néos Marmarás waterfront ☎ 0375 71763 ⏱ Daily, lunch and dinner. Closed midwinter

Toroneos (£)

Bread made to a special recipe by the local baker, unusual dishes especially fish, such as squid stuffed with feta and coriander, fried peppers and pumpkins, friendly service with an interest in the food.

✉ Pefkochóri ☎ 0374 61495 ⏱ Daily, lunch and dinner. Closed winter

Flórina
Okostasis (£)

Smart taverna near main square serving Greek staples and good grills, with local mountain wine.
✉ 25 Martíou 18 ☎ Not known ⏱ Daily, lunch and dinner

Kastoriá
Omonia (£)

Tables outside on busy little square, good place to people-watch and enjoy the basic but well-prepared Greek food. Try the fish soup made from fish caught from the lake.
✉ Plateía Omonoías ☎ 0467 23964 ⏱ Daily, all day

Kavála
Panos Zafira (£££)

Of the many seafood restaurants in town this has established a superior reputation, including unusual items as well as the catches of the day such as mullet or octopus. Near the harbour.
✉ Karaoli Dimitriou 20 ☎ 051 227978 ⏱ Daily, lunch and dinner

Límni Préspa (Préspa Lakes)
Paradosi (£)

One of several fish tavernas in the lovely fishing village of Psarádes, with an idyllic setting and where fish doesn't come any fresher.
✉ Psarádes ⏱ Daily, lunch and dinner

Litóchoro
Damaskinia (£)

Good, bustling family taverna, packed with locals at weekends, serving no-frills

Greek food for hearty appetites. Charcoal grill for fresh meat and fish in summer.

✉ Konstantínou 4 ☎ 0352 81247 🕐 Daily, lunch and dinner

Thessaloníki

Aigli (££)

Superb setting in restored Turkish bath-house where late-night entertainment (musicians, dancers, singers) is as important as the Greco-Turkish food. For a night out, not a romantic dinner.

✉ Kassándrou/Nikoláou ☎ 031 270016 🕐 Thu–Sun 10PM–2:30AM

Aristotelous Ouzerie (££)

Fashionable and tasteful ouzerie hidden down an arcade, serving some of the best Greek dishes you will find, usually with a difference: cuttlefish stuffed with feta or a spicy dip of feta, hot pepper, tomato and oil.

✉ Aristotélous 8 ☎ 031 230762 🕐 Mon–Sat 10AM–2AM, Sun 11AM–6PM

Bextsinar (££)

In fashionable port district of Ladadika, tasteful wood-beamed dining rooms and tasty Middle Eastern menu with emphasis on use of spices and yoghurts.

✉ Katouni 11–13 🕐 Daily 1PM–1:30AM

Kavos (£££)

One of the best, if priciest, of the city's fish restaurants, with a good reputation among locals. Simple décor but the best of the day's catch, impeccably prepared.

✉ Nikifóros Plastíras 59 ☎ 031 430475 🕐 Daily 10AM–2AM

Ta Koubarakia (£)

Very simple Greek grill with friendly waiters, limited menu but generous helpings and set back from busy Egnatía behind a Byzantine church. Very much a neighbourhood place.

✉ Egnatía 140 ☎ 031 271905 🕐 Daily, all day

Krikelas (££)

Thessaloníki favourite for over half a century and one of the best places to taste good regional food, especially game in season, Pelion dishes, Métsovo cheeses.

✉ Ethnikís Antístasis 32 ☎ 031 411289 🕐 Daily 11:30AM–2AM 🚌 5

To Makedoniko (£)

Good, popular, basic Greek taverna in the Eptapirgíou area of the upper town, with limited choice but daily specials and buzzing atmosphere.

✉ Giorgíou Papadopoúlou 32 ☎ 031 627438 🕐 Mon–Sat 9AM–2AM 🚌 23

Ta Nissia (££)

This unmistakable blue and white house in Cycladic style, one street back from the waterfront, contains one of the most imaginative menus around, such as shrimps with bacon, hare with onions, quince and walnut pie.

✉ Proxénou Koromilá 13 ☎ 031 285991 🕐 Daily 12–5PM, 8PM–1AM

Stratis (£)

Modern sea front restaurant with good service, traditional food, extensive wine list, imported beers, generous helpings and especially popular for Sunday lunch.

✉ Níkis 19 ☎ 031 279353 🕐 Daily 12–12

Thanasis (£)

There is no more authentic place than this long-established market taverna, usually packed with local workers seeking the good home-cooked food and terrific atmosphere.

✉ Modiano Market ☎ 031 274170 🕐 Daily 7AM–5AM

Olives and Oil

No one should visit Greece without sampling olives, though those on offer in eating places tend to be limited to black olives in a Greek salad. Visit the markets to see the wide variety available, from different regions and preserved in different ways. Extra virgin olive oil is a good buy to take home and is very reasonably priced.

The Peloponnese

Cheers!

The Greek salutation is *Yammas!* If dining with Greeks, your host will be failing in his duty unless he refills your glass regularly. Glasses are not usually filled right to the brim, as this implies the guest is greedy, and likewise you should not drain your glass completely, for the same reason. Your host will tend to top up your glass when it is about one-third full.

Andrítsaina
Sigouri (£)

Home-made hearty Greek dishes, fresh each day from the kitchen of the lady owner. Specials might include *moussaká* or stuffed tomatoes, and there's wine from the barrel to drink.

✉ **Sofokleos** ☏ **None**
⏱ **Daily, lunch and dinner**

Gýtheio (Yithio)
Kozia (££)

Excellent seafood taverna with wide range of fresh fish along with meat dishes, vegetarian and salads as a cheaper option.

✉ **Vasileos Pavlou 13**
☏ **0733 24086** ⏱ **Daily, lunch and dinner**

Kórinthos (Corinth)
Pantheon (£)

A reliably local place in modern Corinth, where many cater to the passing tourist coach trade and standards can suffer. Good grills, staples such as *moussaká*, generous salads.

✉ **Ethnikis Antistasis**
☏ **0741 25780** ⏱ **Daily, lunch and dinner**

Máni
Lela's (£)

Family-run taverna where mother cooks excellent home recipes, friendly service and views out to sea.

✉ **Sea front, Kardamýli**
☏ **0721 73541** ⏱ **Daily, all day**

Limeni (££)

On the harbour at Areópolis, fish is obviously the forté, with fresh catches, farmed fish kept in tanks till chosen by a customer, and frozen favourites such as squid. Lively spot.

✉ **Liméni harbour, Areópolis**
☏ **0733 51327** ⏱ **Daily, lunch and dinner. Closed midwinter.**

Methóni
Klimateria (££)

One of the best restaurants in the Peloponnese, with lovingly prepared conventional Greek dishes, more imaginative gourmet options, a range of vegetarian meals, fresh fish and lobster, fine wines. It's possible to eat cheaply, but also spend much more extravagantly.

✉ **Plateía Polytechníou**
☏ **0723 31544** ⏱ **Daily, lunch and dinner. Closed in winter**

Monemvasía
Kanoni (££)

Converted 17th-century mansion in the old town, where you are only distracted from the food by the views.

✉ **Main through road of old town** ☏ **0732 61387** ⏱ **Daily, lunch and dinner**

Mykínes (Mycenae)
La Belle Helene (££)

Eat here for a sense of place, as the restaurant is in the hotel that Schliemann stayed in while excavating the site. No surprises on the menu, but better than – and slightly pricier than – the many tourist-trap tavernas that abound.

☏ **0751 76225** ⏱ **Daily, lunch and dinner**

Náfplio
Kakanarakis (£)

In a town where many tavernas are aimed purely at the tourist, this excellent place two streets back from the waterfront offers Greek specials even out of season: rabbit with feta, or squid in a wine sauce are two examples.

✉ **Vasílissis Ólgas 18**
☎ **0752 25371** ⏰ **Daily, lunch and dinner**

Karamanlis (£)

Sea front taverna that retains its Greekness due to its location away from the smarter end of the waterfront. However, the food is good, basic and inexpensive.

✉ **Boumpoulínas 1** ☎ **0752 27668** ⏰ **Daily, 11AM–12AM**

Kipos (£)

Kípos means garden, and this friendly new taverna has a lovely clean garden area off the narrow back street above Plateía Sýntagma, shaded by a lemon tree and some vines. Conventional Greek menu of fish, grills, salads, but well done and worth seeking out.

✉ **Kapodístriou 8** ☎ **None** ⏰ **Daily, lunch and dinner**

Ta Phanaria (£)

Small shaded area by the side of this taverna gives a charming spot for a meal. Good vegetarian options alongside the Greek staples single this out from some of the others in this taverna-lined street.

✉ **Staikopoulos 13** ☎ **0752 27141** ⏰ **Daily, all day**

Zorba's (£)

Unpretentious taverna with friendly service and genuine home-cooking in a street lined with excellent tavernas that are hard to choose between. Zorba's offers *moussaká* light as a feather and other simple dishes cooked by the wife and served by the easy-going husband.

✉ **Staikopoulou 30** ☎ **0752 25319** ⏰ **Daily, lunch and dinner**

Olympía
Kladeos (£)

Lovely riverside setting for old favourite serving seasonal specialities, from game to vegetarian options, and an excellent and substantial *mezédes*.

✉ **Behind railway station**
☎ **0624 23322** ⏰ **Daily 7PM–11PM**

Praxiteles (£)

Justifiably popular eating place for locals and visitors alike, packed inside and out in season: salads, *stifádo*, *souvláki*, daily specials, huge *mezédes*.

✉ **Spiliopoulou 7** ☎ **0624 23570** ⏰ **Daily, lunch and dinner**

Pátra
Evangelatos (£)

On the main street running from the harbour to below the castle, this old-established and very traditional restaurant serves conventional Greek dishes but serves them impeccably.

✉ **Agíou Nikólaou** ☎ **061 277772** ⏰ **Daily, dinner only**

Pharos (££)

Every port has its seafood restaurant named Pharos, or Lighthouse, and this one in Pátra is especially good. There are meat and regular Greek options but the fish is so fresh it would be a shame not to sample something from the daily catch while dining by the harbour.

✉ **Amalías 48** ☎ **061 336500** ⏰ **Daily, lunch and dinner**

Pýlos
Diethnes (££)

Right on the harbour for an ideal eating spot, with fresh fish plucked from the sea that morning, perhaps mullet or swordfish, but more economical meat and Greek favourites, too.

✉ **Paralia** ☎ **None** ⏰ **Daily, all day**

Dining with Children

Visitors with children need not worry about dining as a family. Like other Mediterranean countries, children will dine with adults. If there are several children in a group, they will often be given a table of their own, a charming sight. Foreign visitors with young children can expect to have them fussed over, even taken into the kitchens to help parents enjoy their meal in peace.

Athens & Around

Prices

Approximate prices per person for a one-night stay in high season based on two people sharing a room:

£ = under 10,000dr
££ = 10–20,000dr
£££ = over 20,000dr

Breakfast

The cost of breakfast is not always included in the price of a hotel room, so check when you book. Most hotels serve a cold buffet: expect yoghurt, toast, bread rolls, cold meat, cheese, perhaps pastries. Some hotels may not have breakfast facilities, so check where the nearest cafés are which do serve breakfast.

Central Athens

Achilleas (£)

Newly refurbished and reasonably priced hotel, very close to Sýntagma. All rooms are large and clean, ensuite, with air-conditioning and telephones.

✉ Lekka 21 ☎ 323 3197 Ⓜ Sýntagma (when completed) ✈ Airport bus

Acropolis House (£)

Inexpensive Pláka option in restored mansion though not all rooms have bath. Well-maintained and family-run and very well situated.

✉ Kodrou 6–8 ☎ 322 2344 Ⓜ Sýntagma (when completed) ✈ Airport bus

Acropolis View (£–££)

Good, affordable option on south side of Acropolis but with, naturally, wonderful views of the site. All rooms are ensuite with air-conditioning and telephones, and the hotel is in a quiet location.

✉ Webster 10 ☎ 921 7303 ✈ Airport bus

Adonis (£)

Good, economic hotel in pedestrian street right at the edge of the Pláka and not far from Syntágma. Helpful staff, breakfast room/bar with Acropolis views. The hotel has many regular visitors.

✉ Kodrou 3 ☎ 324 9737 Ⓜ Sýntagma (when completed) ✈ Airport bus

Athenian Inn (££)

Quiet but in fashionable Kolonáki district with views of Lykavittós from some rooms. Traditional furnishings, long established, a favourite of authors and artists but not over-priced.

✉ Charitos 22 ☎ 723 8097 Ⓜ Sýntagma (when completed)

Athens Hilton (£££)

Typical Hilton high standards, and prices, but with an Athenian stamp on it by way of plants, restaurants and as a meeting place for coffee. Convenient for Sýntagma, Benáki Museum and National Gallery, but not the Pláka.

✉ Vasílissis Sofías 46 ☎ 722 0301 Ⓜ Sýntagma (when completed)

Attalos (£)

Simple but clean and well-equipped C-class hotel with friendly service and very convenient for the Pláka, flea market and Monastiráki metro if heading for the ferries. Friendly staff will look after your luggage.

✉ Athínas 29 ☎ 321 2801 Ⓜ Monastiráki

Carolina (£)

A budget option which has seen better days but is perfectly acceptable if funds are limited. Some rooms are ensuite and most are small, but they are kept clean and it is a convenient central base.

✉ Kolokotróni 55 ☎ 324 0944 Ⓜ Monastiráki

Exarchion (£)

Inexpensive choice close to National Archaeological Museum in the lively student area of Exarchía. All rooms are ensuite with air-conditioning, and many have a balcony.

✉ Themistokléous 55 ☎ 380 1256 Ⓜ Omónoia

Grande Bretagne (£££)

Athens' landmark hotel,

where the guest register reads like a roll-call of history. Elegant, marbled interiors, pool, top restaurants, magnificent city views and very expensive.

✉ Plateía Syntágmatos ☎ 333 0000 Ⓜ Sýntagma **(when completed)**

Imperial (£)

Despite the name and location, close to Sýntagma and overlooking Mitrópolis, this is a moderately priced hotel with a friendly staff and clean rooms. Walking distance from most of the main sights.

✉ Mitropóleos 40 ☎ 322 7617 Ⓜ Monastiráki 🚍 Airport bus

King Minos (£–££)

Large and moderately priced hotel close to Omónoia, recently refurbished and having clean rooms, all with air-conditioning and telephones. Bar, restaurant and lounges.

✉ Pireos 1 ☎ 523 1111 Ⓜ Omónoia 🚍 Airport bus

Marble House Pension (£)

Friendly and inexpensive small hotel in quiet location, a short walk from the southern side of the Acropolis. Half of the rooms are ensuite, some have vine-covered balconies, all are clean and the owners extremely helpful.

✉ Zinni 35a ☎ 923 4058 🚍 Airport bus

La Mirage (£)

On Plateía Omonoías but shielded from the noise, all rooms are ensuite with telephone, air-conditioning and mini-bars. Good, well-maintained example of a C-class hotel, with restaurant, bar and lounges. Reasonable rates for those who want to be in among the bustle.

✉ Kotopouli 3 ☎ 523 4755 Ⓜ Omónoia 🚍 Airport bus

Museum (£)

Behind the Archaeological Museum but quiet and well maintained, a good, affordable option if you want to be in this area.

✉ Boumpoulínas 16 ☎ 380 5611 Ⓜ Omónoia

Nefeli (£)

Small and family-run, inexpensive, friendly, modern and spotlessly clean, and convenient for both Pláka and city centre.

✉ Yperidou 16 ☎ 322 8044 Ⓜ Sýntagma **(when completed)** 🚍 Airport bus

Omonia (£)

Budget but acceptable option on Plateía Omonoías, a little worn at the edges but spotlessly clean. All rooms have showers and telephones, some have balconies. Busy and big.

✉ Plateía Omónoia ☎ 523 7211 Ⓜ Omónoia 🚍 Airport bus

Parthenon (£)

Cheap and clean hotel, handy for the Pláka, Sýntagma and, as the name suggests, the Acropolis.

✉ Makri 6 ☎ 923 4594 🚍 Airport bus

Philippos (££)

Good mid-range option for the Makrigianni district, south of the Acropolis and close to several excellent restaurants. All rooms are ensuite, with telephones, TVs and air-conditioning.

✉ Mitseon 3 ☎ 922 3611 🚍 Airport bus

Pláka (££)

Slightly pricier Pláka option, but very smart, clean, modern and bright. Extremely well located close to Mitrópoli, some rooms have views of the Acropolis, as does the roof garden.

✉ Kapnikereas 7 ☎ 322 2096 Ⓜ Monastiráki

Room Rates

All rooms are required by law to have the rates displayed in them, and these are usually inside the door. There will be seasonal variations, and rates can be quoted with or without tax, and with or without breakfast. The owner may offer a discount for a longer stay and for single occupancy of a double room: rates in Greece are per room not per person. Though illegal, smaller hotels may ask you to pay cash, without a receipt, perhaps for a discount.

Passport

Have your passport ready when checking into a hotel, as the owner will need it to help him complete registration forms. Some might ask to keep it until you leave, though normally it will be returned to you within a day or even less.

Royal Olympic (£££)

Large hotel with large rooms, long-established and close to Temple of Olympian Zeus, the Acropolis and Sýntagma. At the cheaper end of its price range, all rooms have TV, telephone and air-conditioning.

✉ Odós Diákou 28 ☎ 922 6411 ⓖ Sýntagma (when completed) 🚌 Airport bus

Tempi (££)

Small and popular budget option for students and those who prefer a friendly atmosphere to frills. Handy for Monastiráki and very central. Clean. Some rooms have showers.

✉ Eólou 29 ☎ 321 3175 ⓖ Monastiráki

Titania (££)

Huge hotel with high standards and reasonable prices, handily placed for both Omónoia and Sýntagma, a short walk from the Pláka and the National Archaeological Museum. Well-equipped rooms, room service, restaurant, roof bar with view of Acropolis. A bonus for drivers is parking space for 400 cars.

✉ Panepistimíou 52 ☎ 330 0111 ⓖ Omónoia & Sýntagma (when completed) 🚌 Airport bus

Around Athens

Akrotírio Soúnio (Cape Sounion)
Aegaeon (£)

Well placed for enjoying Sounion's bay and famous temple. Clean and spacious hotel with good restaurant and moderate prices.

✉ Akrotírio Soúnio ☎ 0292 39200

Marathónas (Marathon)
Hotel Marathon (£)

Close to the Marathon sites and beach, this is a good, clean and rather old-fashioned option for anyone wanting to be near, but not in, Athens. Also a good option as part of a fly-drive holiday.

✉ Timvos Beach ☎ 0294 55122

Pireas
Ideal (£)

Hotels in Pireas can be expensive or seedy, but the Ideal is neither and is situated close to the international ferry ports. It has 29 ensuite rooms, which are also clean and have telephones and air-conditioning. Worth booking ahead if you need to spend a night in Pireas.

✉ Notara 142 ☎ 429 4050 ⓖ Pireas (long walk) 🚌 Airport bus

Lilia (£)

Slightly pricier than the Ideal but in a more pleasant setting away from the noisy waterfronts. Its rooms are just as clean and equally comfortable. The closest harbour is Zea Marina, used by hydrofoils and catamarans to many destinations.

✉ Zeas 131 ☎ 417 9108 ⓖ Pireas (taxi advisable) 🚌 Airport bus

Rafína
Hotel Avra (£)

Very pleasant place for a break in Rafína, some rooms having sea views and all being ensuite with air-conditioning and telephones. Welcoming staff.

✉ Rafína ☎ 0294 22781/3

Central Greece

Aráchova
Apollon (£)
Superb example of a reasonably priced and excellently run little hotel, ideal for exploring Delphi and Parnassós. Clean and pleasant rooms, friendly family owners.

✉ **Delfón 20** ☎ **0267 31427**

Delfoí (Delphi)
Varonos (£)
Very small family-run hotel, ideal for the independent traveller on a budget. Extremely friendly owners, basic but clean rooms, superb views.

✉ **Pávlou and Frederíkis 27** ☎ **0265 82345**

Kalampáka (for Metéora)
Edelweiss (£)
This unlikely name conceals a new and very pleasant hotel in the town of Kalampáka, close to the spectacular Metéora monasteries; some rooms offer distant views of them.

✉ **Venizélou 3** ☎ **0432 23966**

Métsovo
Egnatia (£)
Moderately priced mountain hotel, with traditional stone and woodwork decoration, right on the main street. Some rooms have mountain views, all are ensuite, and the hotel has its own very good restaurant.

✉ **Tosítsa 19** ☎ **0656 41900**

Ioánnina
Olympic (£)
Very good standards in long-established central hotel: bright, clean ensuite rooms with TVs, telephones, air-conditioning and mini-bars.

✉ **Melanidi 2** ☎ **0651 25147**

Pílion (The Pelion)
Archontiko Mousli (£)
One of several restored Pelion mansions in Makrinítsa and other mountain villages, with old furniture and decorated with embroidery and other wall-hangings, these make memorable but expensive places to stay. Booking ahead is recommended, as they are extremely popular.

✉ **Makrinítsa** ☎ **0428 99228**

Eftychia (£)
On the way into the popular beach resort of Ágios Ioánnis, this Pelion-style hotel has sea views and its own restaurant. Closed out of season.

✉ **Ágios Ioánnis** ☎ **0426 31150**

Vergos Mansion (£)
One of the less expensive traditional mansions that has been converted for guesthouse use in the south of The Pelion. Mountain-style décor and views down to the sea.

✉ **Vyzítsa** ☎ **0423 23055**

Zagória
Monodendri Pension (£)
Good-value accommodation in a modern hotel built in traditional Zagorian style. Ensuite rooms and restaurant serving regional food.

✉ **Monodéndri** ☎ **0653 61233**

Saxonis Houses (££)
Cluster of traditional Zagorian mansions converted into elegant if slightly expensive hotel accommodation, retaining some original features such as fireplaces and painted ceilings. In one of Zagória's most attractive mountain villages.

✉ **Megalo Papingo** ☎ **0653 41615**

Grades
All Greek hotel rooms are graded by the Tourist Police in categories with Luxury at the top and then grades from A to E. As is universally found, no rating system is perfect. Hotels are classed according to facilities available, not friendliness or ambiance, so a C-class may seem better to some visitors than a more expensive but shabby B-class.

Northern Greece

The Frontage
It is common practice in Greece to ask to inspect a room before confirming a booking, so don't be afraid to ask. Smart receptions can mask down-at-heel rooms, but equally a very ordinary entrance and reception can lead to a perfectly pleasant hotel. In Athens especially, hotel frontages can be tiny, almost invisible, so first impressions are not always accurate.

Alexandroúpoli
Alkyon (£)
Simple but friendly hotel, tastefully decorated and with good sea views. Inexpensive.
✉ Moudanion 1 ☎ 0551 27465

Chalkidikí
Sani Beach Holiday Resort (£–£££)
The largest holiday complex on the Greek mainland, ideal family choice with watersports, playgrounds, evening entertainment, several restaurants and even its own magazine! Quiet it isn't.
✉ Kassándra ☎ 0374 31231

Skites (£££)
Tasteful, family-run, luxury but low-key hotel, with just a handful of whitewashed wooden-balcony bungalows blending into the wooded grounds. Highly rated restaurant. Good for those who want Chalkidikí but without the brashness of its busy resorts.
✉ Ouranópoli ☎ 0377 71140

Kastoriá
Orestion (£)
Small, inexpensive option in town centre with bar and breakfast room. All rooms are ensuite, well cleaned and comfortable. The owners are friendly and it is just below the Old Town.
✉ Plateía Davaki 1 ☎ 0467 22257

Kavála
Galaxy (££)
Located right by the port and therefore on the expensive side, this is a very good, modern hotel, convenient for ferries and all Kavála's attractions.
✉ Venizélou 27 ☎ 051 224811

Komotiní
Rodopi (£)
Named for the mountains it looks out on, this inexpensive hotel has large, balconied rooms in a converted traditional Thracian mansion.
✉ Ethnarchi Makariou 3 ☎ 0531 35988

Litóchoro
Myrto (£)
Close to the town centre this modern hotel has 32 ensuite rooms, of a good size, helpful staff and a bright restaurant/breakfast room.
✉ Ágios Nikólaos 5 ☎ 0352 81398

Límni Préspa (Préspa Lakes)
Pelekani (£)
Facilities are limited here, but it is clean and cheap, and its setting in the village of Ágios Germanós, close to the Préspa Information Centre, is ideal.
✉ Ágios Germanós ☎ 0385 51442/3

Thessaloníki
Makedonia Palace (£££)
The city's only deluxe hotel is an expensive choice but the most comfortable in town, with excellent food, a quiet location a short walk from the centre, all rooms with balconies and most with sea views, and its own fitness centre, swimming pools and other amenities.
✉ Megálou Aléxandrou 2 ☎ 031 861400

Park (££)
Small, modern hotel, helpful staff, quiet setting but close to the city centre's main sights. Clean, efficient, affordable mid-range hotel.
✉ Dragoúmi 81 ☎ 031 524121

The Peloponnese

Andrítsaina
Theonexia Hotel (£)
The only hotel of any size in this mountain village, where tourists tend to pass through. Facilities are basic but so are prices and the rooms are clean and ensuite. Many also have splendid views of the surrounding mountains.
✉ Andrítsaina ☎ 0626 22219

Gýtheio (Yithio)
Aktaion (£)
Right on the waterfront, this bright and pleasant hotel has been converted from one of the old port mansions. Front rooms have balconies with lovely harbour and sea views.
✉ Vasileos Pavlou 39
☎ 0733 23500

Koróni
Auberge de la Plage (£)
Given the superb views over Koróni's beautiful bay, prices here are surprisingly reasonable. All rooms have balconies and sea views.
✉ Zanga Beach ☎ 0725 22401

The Máni
Guesthouses (£££)
This government-run scheme offers rooms in converted Maniot tower houses dating in origin to the 18th and 19th centuries. Not cheap, but unique accommodation.
✉ EOT Guesthouses, Váthi
☎ 0733 55244

Methóni
Methóni Beach Hotel (£)
Right on the beach, this small (15 ensuite rooms) and well-run hotel is justifiably popular. Also inexpensive, though facilities are basic. It is still sure to be full in season, so booking is advised.
✉ Methóni ☎ 0723 31455

Monemvasía
Malvasia (£££)
There are certain places, and this is one of them, where spending a little bit more is justified by the location. These converted old rooms are in the heart of the Monemvasía fortress, and staying here at night gives the feeling of having closed the drawbridge on the world. Very tasteful rooms, full of wood and embroidery, and a rare chance to feel you have stepped back in time.
✉ Kástro, Monemvasía
☎ 0732 61323

Mystrás (Mistra)
Byzantion (£)
At the foot of the road leading to Mystrás, this simple, inexpensive hotel has 22 ensuite rooms which are small but clean. It is close to the village of Mystrás, and its tavernas.
✉ Mystrás ☎ 0731 93309

Náfplio
Byron (£)
Brightly painted intimate hotel in back street, opposite entrance to Ágios Spirídon church. Thirteen rooms, all with bath and telephone: great personality.
✉ Plateía Agíou Spirídona
☎ 0752 22351

Olympía
Praxiteles (£)
Small and affordable hotels like this are hard to find in the tourist-busy town of Olympía. This is clean and extremely cheap, with 10 ensuite rooms, but do not expect frills. Do expect a good meal if you dine in the family restaurant below, though.
✉ Spiliopoulou 7 ☎ 0624 22592

The Bill
If you plan to, or need to, pay by credit card, make sure first that the hotel accepts your card. Not even all hotels in Athens accept credit cards, as Greeks always prefer to deal in cash no matter how large the wad of money. Outside Athens, where many hotels are small family-run affairs, no credit card facilities may have been arranged.

Arts, Crafts & Jewellery

What to Buy
The best food buys are olive oil and honey, though the latter is not especially cheap. It is especially good, though. Spirits are often at very low prices. Ceramics and leather are also good buys, as are handicrafts such as lace and *flokati*: the hand-woven woollen rugs. There is a big trade in museum copies, and in modern icons. Distinctive Greek items include worry-beads (*komboloi*) and the long-handled copper pots used for making Greek coffee.

Arts and Crafts

Athens and Around
Good junk shops selling artworks, old prints and postcards are to be found at the very far end of Adrianoú, beyond the Tower of the Winds, away from the souvenir shops of the Pláka.

Aidini
Small but distinctive craft workshop and gallery, where the owner makes and sells his own metalwork, including strange fish, hanging airplanes and rather surreal sculptures.
✉ **Nikis 32** ☎ **323 4591/322 6088**

The Athens Gallery
In among the Pláka shops all selling identical items is this stylish gallery representing the work of a handful of contemporary Greek artists: sculptors, painters, potters, jewellery-makers. Expensive but exquisite.
✉ **Pandrossou 14** ☎ **324 6942/894 0217**

Centre of Hellenic Tradition
This arcade between Mitrópoli and the Pláka's Pandrossou houses upstairs a selection of small shops devoted to Greek arts and crafts, including paintings, ceramics, woodwork and icons. It also has an enjoyable and often quiet café.
✉ **Mitropóleos 59/Pandrossou 36** ☎ **321 3023/3842**

Greek Women's Institution
This is an outlet which helps to keep alive the Greek embroidery tradition, providing remote rural and island communities with some benefit from tourism in Greece which they may not otherwise receive.
✉ **Kolokotróni 3** ☎ **325 0524**

Karamikos Mazarakis
In addition to traditional Greek *flokati* rugs and woven kilims, this large shop sells wool and silk rugs from the rest of the world including unusual contemporary rugs based on designs by Dali, Picasso, Magritte and other artists.
✉ **Voulis 31–33** ☎ **322 4932**

Museum of Greek Children's Art
An unusual and charming gift for the art lover can be had here, where prize-winning paintings by Greek children are both on display and for sale. Can you spot the talents of the future?
✉ **Kodrou 9** ☎ **331 2621**

National Welfare Organisation
This excellent scheme offers for sale traditional craftwork and practical items, such as kitchenware, made by rural communities throughout Greece: embroidery, rugs, ceramics, icons.
✉ **Ypatias 6** ☎ **325 0524**

Pyromania
Unlikely name for a fine art and crafts shop, but there are some tasteful examples of handblown glass, ceramics, olive wood carvings, with a small work-shop at the rear where the artist-owner may be at work.
✉ **Kodrou 14** ☎ **325 5288**

Central Greece
Nikos Xaritos
There are plenty of silverwork shops in Ioánnina, but only

a handful of workshops these days. This is one, selling the young owner's handmade plates, cups and decorative items, mainly in silver and brass. Some jewellery for sale, too, on the northern edge of the bazaar area.

✉ **Anexartisías 2, Ioánnina**
☎ **0651 29200**

Nommo
African wooden carvings, decorative boxes, puppets, backgammon sets – a tasteful and good quality ethnic mix.

✉ **Nap. Zerba 28, Ioánnina**
☎ **0651 77321**

Northern Greece
Terra Cotta
Thessaloníki has a lively artistic scene, and this gallery displays some striking work by contemporary artists, both local and from elsewhere in Greece. Closed in midsummer.

✉ **Smyrnis 13, Thessaloníki**
☎ **031 220191**

The Peloponnese
Beselmes Gallery
Artist's own gallery with a wide range of his styles on display, from conventional Greek landscapes to romantic nudes to vivid abstracts.

✉ **Siokou 6, Náfplio**

Genesis
Small ceramic workshop with some tasteful and unusual pottery by owner Katsibootis Panayiotis, who produces them in the workshop on the premises, where you may see him working.

✉ **Kapodistriou 10, Náfplio**
☎ **0752 21884**

Jewellery

Athens and Around
Athens has a long tradition of silversmiths, and a number of shops can be found in the district around Lekka and Praxitelous streets. Some of

these have such huge, garish silver displays that it might be advisable to wear sunglasses! However, there are still some smaller shops which include rather more tasteful items.

Ilias Lalaounis Jewellery Museum
Copies of works by this world-famous Greek jewellery designer, in stylish new museum devoted to his collections. Originals can be ordered, at a price. The Lalaounis Shop can be found at Panepistimíou 6 (☎ 361 1371).

✉ **Karyatidon-Kallisperi 12**
☎ **922 1044**

Nisiotis
Excellent shop specialising in up-market silverware.

✉ **Lekka 23** ☎ **324 4183**

Zolotas
One of Greece's leading jewellers. Even if you cannot afford the items, the jewellery on sale is worth seeing in its own right.

✉ **Panepistimíou 10** ☎ **361 3782**

Northern Greece
Marina
The owner, Marina, once worked for Greece's most celebrated jeweller, Ilias Lalaounis, whose work has influenced her own designs. Not cheap... but more so than her former master.

✉ **Mitropóleos 62, Thessaloníki** ☎ **031 238361**

The Peloponnese
Aelios
Jewellery from a small number of Greek designers, much more stylish than the conventional necklaces and ear-rings on sale in most tourist shops. Imaginatively displayed, and a friendly knowledgeable owner.

✉ **Konstantínou 4, Náfplio**
☎ **0752 28149**

Haggling
Greece is a half-way house between the haggle-free areas of Western Europe and the haggle-filled zones of the Middle East. Haggling over a price should only be done in somewhere like a junk shop, or in the Pláka district in Athens where shop owners inflate prices with a view to offering every visitor, as their special friend, a 'bargain'. In most conventional shops you are only likely to be offered a discount if buying more than one item.

Books, Newspapers, Music & Museum Copies

Opening Hours
Most conventional shops are open on weekday mornings, closing at about 1–2PM for a siesta, then reopening at about 5–6PM for a few hours in the early evening. They will also open on Saturday mornings. In tourist areas they may open Saturday and Sunday too, and at the height of the season shops selling souvenirs and the like may even stay open all day.

Books, Newspapers and Magazines

Athens and Around
The Booknest
Lovely jumble of a bookshop covering hardbacks and paperbacks, old and new, guidebooks and fiction, in many languages.
✉ Panepistimíou 25–9
☎ 323 1703

Compendium
English language books, magazines, guides, fiction, books about Greece, maps and a large second-hand section for exchanging your used paperbacks.
✉ Níkis 25 ☎ 322 1248

Lexis
Good selection of foreign language paperbacks, in a street that is good for bookshops, though mostly of Greek language books.
✉ Akadimías 82 ☎ 384 5823/0844

Raymondos
Very wide range of foreign magazines, and also some books in foreign languages.
✉ Voukourestiou 18 ☎ 364 8189

Central Greece
Athanasias Daktylithos
Good stock of Greek and foreign language newspapers and magazines; newspapers usually available the day after publication.
✉ Pirsinela 14, Ioánnina
☎ 0651 28005

Northern Greece
Molho
Long-established family-run bookstore with a wide range of Greek and foreign language publications, including fiction, books on Thessaloníki and newspapers and magazines.
✉ Tsimiskí 10, Thessaloníki
☎ 031 275271

The Peloponnese
Odyssey
Wide selection of books, newspapers and magazines in several languages, in addition to postcards and conventional souvenirs. Books include guidebooks as well as Greek fiction, or fiction set in Greece, past and present.
✉ Plateía Syntágmatos, Náfplio ☎ 0752 23430

Music

Athens and Around
Museum of Greek Popular Musical Instruments
(► 36). The museum shop sells not instruments but recordings, covering every type of musical tradition from all over Greece. There is also a good stock of books on music and Greek dancing, though mainly in Greek.
✉ Diogenous 1–3 ☎ 325 0198

Museum Copies

Athens and Around
Several of the major museums in Athens sell copies of their most appealing items, and these can range from small and inexpensive to life-size reproductions. Standards are generally very high indeed and the main shops which should be visited are at the National Archaeological Museum (► 21), the Benáki Museum (► 36) and the Museum of Cycladic and Ancient Greek Art (► 36).

Clothes, Food & Drink

Clothes

Athens and Around

The newly pedestrianised Ermoú has a range of Greek and international clothes shops, such as Benetton, Lacoste, Next and Marks and Spencer. More exclusive designer shops can be found in the stylish Kolonáki district, at the foot of Lykavittós.

Yannis Travassaros

This leading Athenian clothes designer has his stylish and inexpensive main shop within the Athens Hilton Hotel.

✉ **Athens Hilton, Leóforos Vassilíssis Sofías** ☎ **722 0201**

Stavros Melissinos

Now a Pláka institution, Melissinos has been making both sandals and poetry since the 1960s. He has made sandals for John Lennon, and sent his poetry to the White House. He will hand-make sandals for you if there is nothing in his cramped and well-stocked quarters that fits the bill, or fits your feet.

✉ **Pandrossou 89** ☎ **321 9247**

Food and Drink

Athens and Around

In Athens, visit the Central Market (► 39) to buy herbs, spices, nuts, olives, cheeses and similar delicacies. It's a good place to visit to buy everything needed for a cheap picnic lunch. This could also be done at the Prisunic Marinopoulos supermarket chain which has a good choice of produce. Look for the large orange 'M' sign.

Aristokratikon

Luxury range of chocolates, nougat, nuts and Turkish delight.

✉ **Karagiórgi Servias 9** ☎ **322 0546**

Asimakopouli

Renowned Athenian patisserie, for those with an extremely sweet tooth: Greeks like their sweets sweeter than most.

✉ **Charíláou Trikoúpi 82** ☎ **361 0092**

Brettos

Well-stocked drink shop in the Pláka district, with own-brand spirits and liqueurs as well as a wide range of Greek drinks such as *ouzo* and Metaxa.

✉ **Kydathinaíon 41** ☎ **323 2110**

Central Greece
Kasa Makis

Wine merchant which sells a world-wide range but also has an extensive stock of good quality Greek wines, of the type that seldom make it onto the limited menus of many restaurants. Also sells a selection of Greek sweets.

✉ **Dimokratías 2, Ioánnina** ☎ **0651 22502**

Northern Greece
Agapitos

Popular sweet and confectionery shop, for those with a sweet tooth.

✉ **Tsimiski 53, Thessaloníki** ☎ **031 279107**

The Peloponnese
Koroni

Superior drink shop stocking international brands but also a range of up-market Greek wines.

✉ **Amalías 6, Náfplio**

Supermarkets

Greece has a long tradition of the village shop which sells everything, so if directed to the 'supermarket' do not necessarily expect the huge American-style shopping experience. An experience it may be, as the shopkeeper delves into the dusty stock to find what you want – and often succeeding – but not on the American scale. Supermarkets are also mini-markets, especially in tourist areas, again selling everything you might possibly need.

Museums

Children in Greece

Greeks love children and children are made welcome almost anywhere, although the number of attractions outside of Athens that are specially aimed at children is negligible. Children play on the beach, they play together in rural villages, and the need for organised entertainment for them is limited. You may find a small funfair in some towns, or an occasional travelling circus, but otherwise children do what the adults do... only more noisily.

Athens and Around
Goulandrís Natural History Museum

This excellent museum in Kifissiá tackles the problems of the environment, some of which can be caused by tourism – a lesson that travellers are never too young to learn. There are also extensive collections of Greek fauna and flora, including mammals such as bears and wolves which few visitors will ever see in the wild.

☒ Levidou 13 ☎ 808 6405
🕐 Sat–Sun 9–2. Closed public hols 🚇 Kifissiá

Hellenic Children's Museum

This new venture is close to the Museum of Greek Folk Art (► 36), and although small and a little improvised as yet, its maze of rooms includes work rooms, play rooms and displays on such subjects as the building of the new Athens Metro lines. Although some of the staff speak English and welcome children of all ages and nationalities, advance notice for visits by non-Greek speaking children is advisable.

☒ Kydathinaíon 14 ☎ 331 2995 🕐 Mon, Wed 9:30–1:30, Fri 9:30–1:30, 5–8, Sat–Sun 10–1. Closed Tue, Thu 🚇 Sýntagma (when completed)

Museum of Greek Children's Art

This small and lively museum has displays of art including imaginative sculptures, but also tables and materials for children to use. There are some organised classes which welcome visiting children, and with a little advance warning an English-speaking teacher can be made available too, though

other languages are more difficult to arrange.

☒ Kodrou 9 ☎ 331 2621
🕐 Tue–Sat 10–2, Sun 11–2. Closed Mon & public hols
🚇 Sýntagma (when completed)

Museum of Greek Musical Instruments

While it is not possible to actually play any of the instruments in this valuable collection (► 36), it is however possible to listen to most of them on headphones provided. Videos show how various instruments are made and played.

☒ Diogenous 1–3 ☎ 325 0198 🕐 Tue, Thu–Sun 10–2, Wed 12–6. Closed Mon & public hols 🚇 Monastiráki

The War Museum of Greece

Outside the museum (► 38) are airplanes that can be climbed up to and peered into, and a range of weaponry that visitors can get a close look at. Some of the dioramas inside are also interesting to children.

☒ Leóforos Vasilíssis Sofías 22/Rizari 2 ☎ 729 0543
🕐 Tue–Fri 9–2; Sat–Sun 9:30–2. Closed Mon & public hols
🍴 Café (£) 🚌 234

Northern Greece
Museum of the Macedonian Struggle

From a child's point of view the most interesting area is the basement, where several large dioramas give a vivid portrayal of life for the resistance fighters. Upstairs, several smaller models can be illuminated and there is plenty of weaponry to look at.

☒ Proxénou Koromilá 23
☎ 031 229778 🕐 Tue–Fri 9–2, Sat–Sun 11–2, Wed evening 6–8. Closed Mon & public hols

Outdoor Pursuits

Fun Excursions

Athens and Around
Lykavittós
Though children are not normally gripped for long by panoramic views over cities, such as you get from the top of Lykavittós (➤ 33), they will probably enjoy the journey up there if you take them on the funicular.
✉ **Ploutarchou** ⓘ **Daily 8AM–10PM**

Pireas and the Islands
A good day out is to make a day trip to one or more of the Argo-Saronic islands. An early start will mean a ride on the Metro to Pireas, and then the excitement of a journey on one of the hydrofoils to Aígina (Aegina), Póros, Spétses or Ýdra (Hydra).
🚇 **Pireas**

Central Greece
Ioánnina
Take a boat-ride across to the island of Nisí, and a bus or taxi ride out to tour the Pérama Caves.

The Peloponnese
Kalávryta Railway
A journey on the mountain railway, climbing from Diakoftó into the Peloponnesian mountains, is a thrilling ride for children and adults alike.
☎ **513 1601 for timetable details** ⓘ **All year. Several trains daily in each direction**

Beach Resorts

Central Greece
Párga
One of the best holiday resorts on the west coast, with plenty of watersports and several good beaches.

Northern Greece
Chalkidikí
One of the busiest of Greek holiday areas, and most resorts have plenty of activity to keep children happy, with good beaches, some of the cleanest waters in Greece, and lots of watersports and other children.

The Peloponnese
Koróni and Methóni
Two great seaside resorts, with Koróni having one of the best beaches in Greece, ideal for swimming and collecting some of the thousands of multi-coloured stones scattered on the beach.

Tólo
Parents might prefer the more sophisticated air of Náfplio, but this busy resort just along the coast is a far better destination for family holidays.

Other Places to Visit

Athens and Around
National Gardens
In addition to simply exploring the gardens (➤ 32), perhaps looking for small ponds where fish and terrapins live, there is also a Children's Library in the centre of the gardens.
ⓘ **Library closed Mon & public hols**

The Peloponnese
Corinth Canal
Interest soon wanes, but the first sight of the dramatic canal is breathtaking, and with plenty of parking space, cafés and souvenir shops, the area around the road which crosses the canal is a good place to take a break from driving.

Swimming
Greek children learn to swim at an early age, and love showing off by performing back flips, underwater handstands and other daredevil tricks. Beaches are generally very safe for children of all ages, but lifeguards are rare so do keep an eye on children who might wander off with the excitement of making new friends. Take the usual protections against sunburn and dehydration, and also against injury from sea urchins or jellyfish in some areas.

Nightlife, Theatre, Sport

Late Nights

There has been a lot of controversy in Greece in the last few years over the Greeks' love of the very late night. Workers and even schoolchildren have been falling asleep during the day, after being awake till the early hours of the morning. The government tried to bring in measures to curb this, by imposing a 2AM close-down on clubs, restaurants and entertainment venues; people merely continued partying by other means. Be assured that if you are a night owl, then you will be at home in Greece.

Publications

Athens has several English-language listings magazines, such as *Athens Today* and *Scope Weekly*, providing up-to-date information on what's happening in the city. There are also weekly and daily English-language newspapers, and a German-language weekly. There are Greek-language publications too, available at most newsagents and kiosks. If in difficulty, try around Sýntagma Square. The more cultural monthly magazine, *The Athenian*, also has news of movies, galleries, music and other entertainment options.

Casinos

Athens and Around
Casino
On top of Mount Parnes, an hour's drive north of Athens, is one of Europe's biggest casinos.
☎ 246 9111 🕒 Closed Wed

Northern Greece
Casino Pórto Cárras
✉ Néos Marmarás ☎ 0375 72500

Regency Casino Thessaloníki
✉ Hyatt Regencey Hotel
☎ 031 491234

Xánthi Casino
☎ 0541 70900

The Peloponnese
Club Hotel Loutráki
✉ Posidonos 48, Loutráki
☎ 0744 66501

Theros International
✉ Hotel Porto Rio, Pátra
☎ 061 993997

Festivals

Each summer sees the Athens Festival, including all the major art forms, and incorporating some music and theatrical performances held in the theatre at Epídavros as well as the Théatro Iródou Attikoú (Herodes Atticus Theatre) below the acropolis. Get a current programme, and book tickets, at the box office.

Athens and Epídavros Festival Box Office
✉ Stadiou 4 ☎ 322 1459

Movies

Athens has a few dozen cinemas in and around the centre, and in summer these are increased with the arrival of temporary open-air screens on vacant lots. You can see new movies here as quickly as anywhere in Europe, and usually in the original language with Greek sub-titles added.

Music

There are countless music venues in Athens, from classical concert halls (see some suggestions under Theatre) to *rembétika* clubs tucked away all over the city. There are jazz clubs, blues clubs, rock venues, discos, dance clubs and innumerable places putting on traditional Greek music, whether for those who prefer the safety of a popular tourist venue or those who want the real thing in the company of Athenians. Buy one of the many listings magazines such as *Scope Weekly* for further details. Some suggestions include:

Athens and Around
Half Note Jazz Club
Lively jazz club in the Mets area.

✉ Trivonianou 17 ☎ 921 3310

Taverna Kalokerinos
Very much a tour group venue in the Pláka, but noisy nights where the music and dancing is more important than the food.

✉ Kekropos 10 ☎ 323 2054

Sound and Light
The Acropolis is on show from the theatre on Filopáppou Hill, clearly marked from the entrance opposite the southern slopes of the Acropolis.

☎ 322 1459 🕐 1 Apr–31 Oct. **English nightly at 9PM, German at 10PM on Tue & Fri, French at 10PM all other nights**

Northern Greece
Mylos
The big entertainment centre in the city is near the port in a converted mill. It contains restaurant, bars, café, disco, music clubs, galleries, cinema and theatre. Greek and international acts play here, and at weekends it is standing room only, well into the night.

✉ Andreadou Giorgiou 25, Thessaloniki ☎ 031 516945

Theatre

Athens and Around
Dora Stratou Dance Theatre
This small open-air theatre at the foot of the Filopáppou Hill helps keep Greek tradi-tional dance alive by putting on nightly performances throughout the summer tourist season. These are very popular and booking is advisable.

✉ Filopáppou ☎ 324 4395

Mégaron Athens Concert Hall
This bright new building was opened in 1991 and has ballet, opera and classical music, including performances by the Athens State Orchestra and visiting companies.

✉ Vasílissis Sofías and Kokkáli ☎ 728 2333

National Theatre
These are generally Greek-language productions of international dramas, though occasionally a visiting theatre group will perform in their own language. Foreign visitors might prefer to look for one of the dance or opera productions, also frequent.

✉ Agíou Konstantínou 22 ☎ 523 3322

Pallas Theatre
Venue for major rock concerts, but classical performances too.

✉ Voukourestiou 1 ☎ 322 8275

Northern Greece
Thessaloníki
Thessaloníki has two theatres, the winter and summer homes of the State Theatre of Northern Greece, the *Kratikó Théatro*. The indoor venue is called the State Theatre, slightly east of the White Tower on the waterfront, and outdoors in summer performances transfer to the Forest Theatre (*Théatro Dásous*), on the hilltop east of the Upper City.

☎ 031 223785 (winter); 031 218092 (summer)

Skiing

Central Greece
Parnassós Ski Centre
Small by Western European standards but nevertheless providing 20 slopes and decent facilities.

☎ 0234 22689/22493

Pilion Ski Centre
Not quite as high as Parnassós but a popular centre, near Chánia.

☎ 0421 25696

Love of Sport
Football remains Greece's number one sporting obsession, but in recent years it has fast been caught up by basketball, since the Greek team won the 1987 European Championships. Don't be surprised if you find it hard to get served in a bar or taverna when all eyes are glued to sport on TV. An interest in, and knowledge of, soccer or basketball will win you instant friends.

Festivals & Events – What's On When

Public Holidays

On Greece's annual public holidays you will find almost everywhere closed, including sites and museums, government offices, banks and post offices and many shops and restaurants. Some private businesses will remain open in busy holiday areas in summer, but even then don't assume you'll be able to buy everything you need. Travelling will also be difficult, so check before you set out. There are also many local feasts where private businesses will close but government ones will stay open... or should do. The public holidays are 1 and 6 January, and 25 March, first Monday in Lent, Easter Friday–Monday, 1 May, Whit Monday, 15 August, 28 October, 25 and 26 December.

1 January – New Year's Day

Known throughout Greece as St Basil's Day, when presents are exchanged and a special bread (*vassílopitta*) is baked. This contains a coin, bringing good fortune to the person who receives it.

6 January – The Epiphany

The Baptism of Christ, when fonts and outdoor bodies of water are blessed. In some seaside towns the priest will throw a cross into the harbour for the young men to try to retrieve.

25 March – Independence Day and The Annunciation or *Evangelismós*

A joint religious and secular feast, one of the biggest in the year. Independence Day parades celebrate the 1821 War of Independence against the centuries of Turkish rule, the biggest being, naturally, in Athens, while the Feast of the Annunciation sees a celebration of the news given to the Virgin Mary that she was to become the Mother of Christ.

23 April – St George's Day (Ágios Giórgios)

St George is the patron saint of shepherds so this is widely celebrated in rural communities, the most notable being at Aráchova (► 52) with races and feasts.

1 May – May Day or *Protomagiá*

Also known as Labour Day, the traditional day for families to picnic in the countryside. Wreaths made from wild flowers are taken home to be hung over doors, on balconies and on boats, to protect against evil. There they will stay until 24 June, the feast of St John. More public celebrations include workers' parades.

21 May – Feast of Saints Konstantinos and Eleni (Ágios Konstantínos kai Agía Eléni)

Two important Orthodox saints, and name-day celebrations (► panel) for those named after them. Also the time for fire-walking ceremonies at Lagkadás near Thessaloníki. There have been attempts to suppress these ancient rites in recent years, but they appear to be surviving.

24 June – St John's Day (Ágios Ioánnis)

St John the Baptist is a significant saint, and the many boys named Ioánnis in his honour will also be celebrating this day. Wreaths made on 1 May can now be safely burned, with summer at last arrived.

29 June – Feast of the Holy Apostles Saints Peter and Paul (Ágioi Apóstoloi Pétros kai Pávlos)

A big day, as is the evening before, when the wreaths made at the picnics on 1 May will be burnt in bonfires – the danger from evil successfully passed. It is also a widely celebrated name day for those called Pétros and Pávlos.

17 July – Saint Marina (Agía Marína)

Marína is the protector of crops so her feast day is a big cause for celebration in farming communities.

18–20 July – Feast of the Prophet Elijah (Profítis Ilías)

Many hilltop monasteries are named after the prophet, and this is where pilgrimages will be made and services held. The biggest celebration takes place at the chapel at the top of the highest peak of the Távgetos mountain range.

6 August – Feast of the Transfiguration (Metamórfosi)

Celebrated at churches named for this feast.

15 August – Feast of the Assumption of the Blessed Virgin Mary (Apokoímisis tis Panagías)

Very important day when Greeks return home to their villages – not a good day for tourists to be travelling without a booking as ferries to the islands are often full and on the mainland many hotels will be fully booked around this date. It is, however, a very good day for attending services, followed by feasting, drinking and dancing late into the night.

8 September – Birth of the Virgin Mary (Génnisis tis Theotókou)

The Virgin Mary is highly revered in the Greek Orthodox Church, and her birth is a big religious feast.

26 October – Saint Dimítrios (Ágios Dimítrios)

The patron saint of Thessaloníki sees processions and a large gathering at the church dedicated to him, the largest in Greece. There is also extensive sampling of the first of the summer wine.

28 October – Óchi Day

Commemorates the day in 1940 when Greek General Metaxa gave a defiant one-word response, *Óchi* (No), to Mussolini's demand for access to Greek ports. In fact his response was longer, and was given in French at that, but the Greeks celebrate the gist of it. Schools and military colleges mount parades and in Athens Sýntagma is the focus of the celebrations.

30 November – Feast of St Andrew (Ágios Andréas)

Widely celebrated but especially in Pátra, in the cathedral dedicated to the saint.

6 December – Feast of St Nicholas (Ágios Nikólaos)

The patron saint of seafarers is naturally honoured at the many seaside churches named after him.

25 December – Christmas Day (Christoúgenna)

Not as important as Easter in Greek eyes, nor as commercial as in many countries – more a day for church services and private celebrations.

26 December – The Meeting of the Virgin's Entourage (Sýnaxis tis Theotókou)

Continues the holy celebrations in the vein of Christmas Day.

31 December – New Year's Eve

Children traditionally sing Christmas carols within their village or neighbourhood, and adults get together with friends and family to celebrate as elsewhere in the world.

Name Days

Though children still celebrate their birthdays, Greek adults celebrate their name days instead. That is, the feast of the saint after whom they are named. In some places this can mean everyone who bears the same name deciding to get together and celebrate by way of a big party, to which all are invited. If this is an open party, visitors will be equally welcome, with perhaps a nominal payment made to cover the food and drink.

Travelling at Easter

If Greek families only get together once during the year, it will be at Easter. This means many Athenians will leave the city to return to their original village or island homes. The exodus increases as Easter weekend approaches, so if you need to travel during this period be sure to book tickets well in advance. Don't forget that transport will also be very busy immediately after Easter Monday.

Moveable Feasts

In addition to the festivals and events listed on the previous two pages, there are a number of Greek celebrations which are held at different times each year, determined by the Orthodox calender.

Carnival (Karnaváli)

While Greece's Carnival celebrations are not as Bacchanalian as in some countries, they are certainly enthusiastically enjoyed. Parades are common, and parties too – both public and private. The best-known celebrations are in Pátra, including a chariot parade and a Saturnalia. In Athens the rather tamer custom is to hit each other on the head with plastic hammers.

Carnival takes place during the three weeks prior to Lent, with the biggest celebrations saved for the Sunday immediately before the start of Lent: seven weeks before Easter weekend.

Easter

Easter is by far the biggest event in the Greek calendar, and anyone who has not visited Greece at that time should certainly try to do so one year. Check the dates first, though, as the complicated way of calculating the Orthodox Easter differs from the complicated way of calculating Easter in the rest of Europe! Greek Easter can fall anything up to three weeks before or after other Easters, and every few years they will coincide.

Churches will be open prior to Easter weekend as people prepare for the festivities. The bier on which Christ's body will be laid is decorated with flowers, and in some places these can be hugely elaborate. On Friday evening this is carried through the streets.

Visitors will be quite welcome to join in the procession.

On Easter Saturday evening the main church service takes place. This has a dramatic climax when each church is plunged into darkness, reminding us of Christ's body in the tomb. Then as midnight approaches the priest emerges from behind the altar carrying a single candle with which he lights the candles of the parishioners, who in turn pass the light on to those behind them and outside the church. The church lights will be switched on again, the bells will be rung and fireworks set off – in some cases ship's flares and even dynamite. People will greet each other by saying *Christós Anésti* (Christ is Risen), the reply being *Alithós Anésti* (Truly He is Risen).

After the service people will endeavour to carry their candle home without it going out, to ensure good fortune for the rest of the year. They will then enjoy the *magarítsa* soup, made only at Easter from eggs, lemon, rice and offal from the Paschal lamb. The rest of the lamb will be roasted on Easter Sunday, when families get together for big celebrations. In the morning hard-boiled eggs painted red will be handed round, and these are cracked against each other to see who will have the best fortune in the forthcoming 12 months.

Whit

Seven weeks after Greek Easter, Whit Sunday and Monday are also celebrated, with Monday being a national holiday. Again, expect to see parades and family get-togethers, although not on the scale of Carnival or Easter.

Practical Matters

GMT	Greece	Germany	USA (NY)	Netherlands	Spain
12 noon	→ 2PM	→ 1PM	← 7AM	→ 1PM	→ 1PM

BEFORE YOU GO

WHAT YOU NEED

- ● Required
- ○ Suggested
- ▲ Not required

	UK	Germany	USA	Netherlands	Spain
Passport/National Identity Card	●	●	●	●	●
Visa	▲	▲	▲	▲	▲
Onward or Return Ticket	▲	▲	▲	▲	▲
Health Inoculations (tetanus and polio)	○	○	○	○	○
Health Documentation (reciprocal agreement document, ➤ 123, Health)	●	●	▲	●	●
Travel Insurance	●	●	●	●	●
Driving Licence (EU or International)	●	●	●	●	●
Car Insurance Certificate (if own car)	●	●	●	●	●
Car registration document (if own car)	●	●	●	●	●

WHEN TO GO

Athens

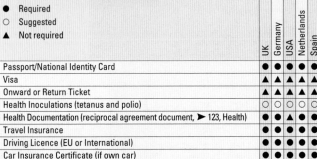

| | High season |
| | Low season |

14°C	14°C	16°C	20°C	25°C	30°C	33°C	33°C	29°C	24°C	18°C	15°C
JAN	FEB	MAR	APR	MAY	JUN	JUL	AUG	SEP	OCT	NOV	DEC

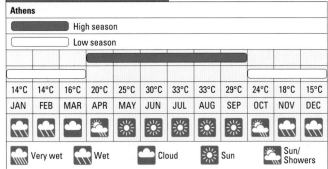

Very wet   Wet   Cloud   Sun   Sun/Showers

TOURIST OFFICES

In the UK
National Tourist
Organisation of Greece
(NTOG)
4 Conduit Street
London W1R 0DJ
☎ 0171 734 5997
Fax: 0171 287 1369

In the USA
National Tourist
Organisation of Greece
(NTOG)
645 Fifth Avenue
New York NY10022
☎ 212/421 5777
Fax: 212/826 6940

611 West Sixth Street
Suite 2198
Los Angeles
CA92668
☎ 213/626 6696
Fax: 213/489 9744

POLICE 100	
FIRE 100	
AMBULANCE 100	
TOURIST POLICE 171 (Athens only)	

WHEN YOU ARE THERE

ARRIVING

Olympic Airways, the Greek national airline, offers the widest choice of scheduled flights to Athens and also flies to Thessaloníki from some countries. For those arriving by sea, there are regular car and passenger ferries between Ancona, Bari and Brindisi in Italy, and Igoumenítsa and Pátra on the mainland.

Ellinikón International Airport, Athens Kilometres to city centre	**Journey Times**	
	🚇	N/A
	🚌	30 minutes
10 kilometres	🚗	20 minutes

Thessaloniki Airport Kilometres to city centre	**Journey times**	
	🚇	N/A
	🚌	50 minutes
16 kilometres	🚗	30 minutes

MONEY

The monetary unit of Greece is the drachma (dr). Notes are in denominations of dr10,000, 5000, 1000, 500 and 100, and coins of dr100, 50, 20, 10, 5, 2 and 1. Foreign currencies and travellers' cheques can be exchanged at all banks, and bureaux de change and some banks accept the major credit cards (Visa, Mastercard, American Express, Diners Club) for cash advances. However, only the larger and more expensive hotels, shops and restaurants will accept payment by credit card: cash is still the preferred method of payment in Greece.

TIME

 Mainland Greece is two hours ahead of Greenwich Mean Time (GMT+2) and one hour ahead of the rest of Western Europe, but from late March to late September, summer time (GMT+3) operates.

CUSTOMS

 YES

Goods Obtained Duty Free Inside the EU or Goods Bought Outside the EU (Limits):
Alcohol (over 22° vol): 1L *or*
Fortified wine, sparkling wine or other liquors: 2L *and*
Still table wine: 2L
Cigarettes: 200 *or*
Cigars: 50 *or*
Tobacco: 250gms
Perfume: 60cc
Toilet water: 250cc
Goods Bought Duty and Tax Paid Inside the EU (Guidance Levels):
Alcohol (over 22° vol): 10L *and*
Fortified wine: 20L *and*
Wine (max 60L sparkling): 90L *and* Beer: 110L
Cigarettes: 800 *and*
Cigars: 200 *and*
Tobacco: 1kg
Perfume and Toilet Water: no limit
Visitors must be 17 or over.

 NO

Drugs, (medication, including codeine, must have a doctor's certificate), plants in soil. Art and antiquities must be declared on entry so that they can be re-exported.

119

EMBASSIES AND CONSULATES

 UK
01 723 6211/9 (A)
031 278006 (T)

 Germany
01 369 4111 (A)
031 236315 (T)

 USA
01 721 2951/9 (A)
031 266121 (T)

 Netherlands
01 723 9701 (A)
031 227477 (T)

 Spain
01 721 4885 (A)

(A) = Athens;   (T) = Thessaloníki

WHEN YOU ARE THERE

TOURIST OFFICES

Ellinikos Organismos Tourismou (EOT)
● (National Tourist Organisation of Greece)
PO Box 1017
Odós Amerikis 2
10564 Athens
☎ 01 322 3111
Fax: 01 325 2895

Local Information Offices in Athens:
● EOT Information Desk
Karayeorgi Servias 2
(inside National Bank building)
☎ 01 322 2545

● EOT Information Desk
General Bank of Greece
Ermou 1
Syntagma
☎ 01 325 2667/8

● Hellenic Chamber of Hotels
Information Desk
National Bank Building
Karayeorgi Servias 2
☎ 01 323 7193

● East Terminal
Athens Airport
☎ 01 969 9500

Thessaloníki:
● EOT Tourist Office
Plateia Aristotelous 8
☎ 031 271888

Olympía:
● Municipal Tourist Office
Praxitelous Kondili (near the bus stops)
☎ 0621 23100/23125
There are offices in most other large towns and cities in Greece.

NATIONAL HOLIDAYS

J	F	M	A	M	J	J	A	S	O	N	D
2	(1)	1(3)	(1)	1	1		1		1		2

1 Jan	New Year's Day
6 Jan	Epiphany
Late Feb/early Mar	Shrove Monday
25 March	Greek Independence Day
Mar/Apr	Good Fri, Easter Sun and Mon
1 May	May Day or Labour Day
3 June	Holy Spirit Day
15 Aug	Assumption of the Virgin
28 Oct	Óchi Day
25 Dec	Christmas Day
26 Dec	St Stephen's Day

Shops and some restaurants close on public holidays, and often on the afternoon before and the morning after a religious holiday. In tourist areas, however, tavernas and some shops will open.

OPENING HOURS

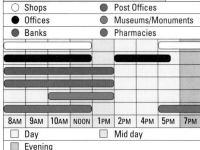

○ Shops	● Post Offices
● Offices	● Museums/Monuments
● Banks	● Pharmacies

| 8AM | 9AM | 10AM | NOON | 1PM | 2PM | 4PM | 5PM | 7PM |

| □ Day | □ Mid day |
| ▨ Evening | |

In addition to the times in the chart above (which are given as a guide only), most shops and supermarkets in tourist areas may open longer hours. Pharmacies are closed on Saturday and Sunday.

In large towns, post offices may stay open longer hours than shown and may open on Saturday morning. Exchange bureaux are open until 10PM.

It is always advisable to check the opening times of museums and sites locally as these vary from summer to winter and sometimes from early summer to peak season.

**DRIVE ON THE
RIGHT**

**TOILETS
BASIC**

PUBLIC TRANSPORT

 Internal Flights Domestic flights are operated by Olympic Airways (☎ 01 966 6666), and it is possible to make connections at Athens and Thessaloníki to several provincial airports and to the Greek Islands. Olympic Airways domestic flight tickets are non-transferable. All Olympic Airways internal flights are non smoking.

 Trains Greek trains are cheaper than buses, but also tend to be slower, and the network is restricted. However there are now some faster inter-city trains to compete with the usually superior bus services. Timetables can be obtained from NTOG offices but are often subject to late changes. Carriages can be very crowded.

Buses Greek buses, operated by KTEL, are the best way to travel, being cheap and reasonably regular. NTOG offices provide timetables of services from Athens and a route map is available from the EOT in Athens. Long-distance tickets may be purchased in advance; other tickets are paid for on the bus. Smoking is banned on all buses.

 Ferries and Hydrofoils Many mainland towns have services to certain islands, the main port being Pireas in Athens. There are several different harbours in Pireas, quite some distance apart, and it is important to know from which harbour your ferry will be leaving. An up-to-date timetable can be obtained from the NTOG.

Urban Transport Services in the cities and main towns are frequent and cheap. Athens has buses, trolleys and a metro (a second metro line is currently being built). Flat-fare tickets must be bought in advance from kiosks and validated once on board. In Thessaloníki, tickets are paid for on the bus, from the conductor or a machine.

CAR RENTAL

Vehicles hired from the major rental firms tend to be newer and safer than those from local agencies, but you should always check the insurance cover. The minimum rental age ranges from 21 to 25. An International driving licence is not required for EU licence holders.

TAXIS

 Greek taxis are good value and it is common to book them for longer journeys as well as short ones. They run on a share basis and drivers are allowed to stop to pick up other passengers going in the same direction. Check that the taxi is metered, or agree the fare in advance.

DRIVING

 Speed limit on motorways and dual carriageways: **100kph**

 Speed limit outside built-up areas: **80kph**

 Speed limit in urban areas: **50kph**

 Must be worn in front seats at all times and in rear seats where fitted. Children under 12 years must not sit in the front seat.

 Random breath testing: drinking and driving can be punishable by a prison sentence and your car permanently confiscated. Blood alcohol level of more than 0.05 per cent is an offence.

 Unleaded petrol is available though not all petrol stations stock it. The main grades are 'super', the equivalent to 4-star and 'regular' (2-star). Petrol stations exist in all but the smallest villages and are normally open seven days a week. Fuel is expensive and few garages take credit cards.

 It is compulsory to carry a first-aid kit, a fire extinguisher and a warning triangle in any car in Greece.
If you break down and have proof of AA, RAC or similar membership, you will be entitled to free roadside assistance from ELPA, the Greek national breakdown service (☎ 01 779 1615).
In emergency dial 104.

PERSONAL SAFETY

Greece is one of the safest countries in Europe, but crime is on the increase, especially in crowded places. Report any problems to the Tourist Police, who can often speak several European languages.

- Leave money and valuables in the hotel safe. Carry only what you need and keep it hidden.

- Women travelling alone can expect some minor harassment from *kamáki*, men on the lookout for a sexual encounter. Be firm in your refusal.

- Do not touch stray dogs. If bitten get medical help.

Tourist Police assistance:
☎ **171**

TELEPHONES

International Direct Dialling is available throughout Greece. Calls can be made using a phone card in a telephone booth. Cards can be bought from kiosks, OTE offices and some shops, in units of 100, 500 and 1,000. Alternatively, you can make calls from street kiosks which have metered phones and pay at the end of the call, although connections tend to be poor.

International Dialling Codes

From Greece to:	
UK:	**00 44**
Germany:	**00 49**
USA:	**00 1**
Netherlands:	**00 31**
Spain:	**00 34**

POST

Post Offices
Post offices are identified by a yellow 'OTE' sign. Queues can be long and slow and if you want only stamps (*ghramatósima*) for post-cards, try kiosks or shops selling cards. Post boxes are yellow: use the slot marked *Exoterico* for overseas mail. Post offices are generally open Monday to Friday 8–2.

ELECTRICITY

The power supply in Greece is: 220 volts AC, 50 Hz.

Sockets accept two-round-pin continental-style plugs.
Visitors from the UK require a plug adaptor and US visitors will need a transformer for appliances operating on 100–120 volts.

TIPS/GRATUITIES

Yes ✓ No ✗		
Restaurants (service included)	✓	100 dr
Cafés/Bar Service	✓	100dr or 10%
Taxis	✓	change
Tour guides	✓	200dr
Porters	✓	1–200dr
Chambermaids	✓	100dr per day
Hairdressers	✓	200dr or 10%
Cloakroom attendants	✓	100dr
Toilets	✗	

PHOTOGRAPHY

What to photograph: Greece has more ancient sites than any other European country and photography is free (for hand-held cameras) on most sites. The Greek people also like to be photographed, but it is polite to ask permission.

Where you need permission to photograph: in some museums and always if using a tripod. Never photograph near military installations.

Where to buy film: film is expensive, but major brands are widely available in all tourist areas.

HEALTH

Insurance

EU citizens are entitled to, on production of an E111 form, free emergency treatment in Greek state hospitals, but these are overcrowded and underfunded, and any other treatment must be paid for (obtain receipts). Medical insurance is therefore recommended, and is essential for non-EU nationals.

Dental Services

Dental treatment is not available free of charge and should be covered by your private medical insurance. Check with the Tourist Police or at your hotel for the name of the nearest dentist. Have a check-up before leaving home.

Sun Advice

The heat of the sun is the biggest health risk in Greece. It is very hot in summer, especially in August when the temperature in Athens can reach 40°C. You should keep out of the noon sun, and keep sensitive areas covered, in addition to wearing sunglasses, a hat and a high protection sunscreen.

Drugs

Pharmacies (*farmakeío*), indicated by a green cross sign, can give advice and prescriptions for common ailments. If you need prescription drugs, take the exact details from home. Note that codeine is banned in Greece and you can be fined for carrying it.

Safe Water

Tap water is chlorinated and is regarded as safe to drink, but if you prefer mineral water it is cheap to buy and is widely available. Drink plenty of water during the hot weather.

CONCESSIONS

Students/Youths An International Student Identity Card (ISIC) can provide travel discounts and cheap entry into museums and sites. There are some Youth Hostels in mainland Greece, well situated for the main areas of interest, which provide cheap basic accommodation for members of the Greek Association of Youth Hostels, ☎ 01 323 4107, and there are also YMCA and YWCA hostels in Athens and Thessaloníki.

Senior Citizens The Greek tourist season runs from May to October, and with many hotels closing for the winter, there are few opportunities for cheap holidays out of season.

CLOTHING SIZES

Greece	UK	Rest of Europe	USA	
46	36	46	36	Suits
48	38	48	38	Suits
50	40	50	40	Suits
52	42	52	42	Suits
54	44	54	44	Suits
56	46	56	46	Suits
41	7	41	8	Shoes
42	7.5	42	8.5	Shoes
43	8.5	43	9.5	Shoes
44	9.5	44	10.5	Shoes
45	10.5	45	11.5	Shoes
46	11	46	12	Shoes
37	14.5	37	14.5	Shirts
38	15	38	15	Shirts
39/40	15.5	39/40	15.5	Shirts
41	16	41	16	Shirts
42	16.5	42	16.5	Shirts
43	17	43	17	Shirts
36	8	34	6	Dresses
38	10	36	8	Dresses
40	12	38	10	Dresses
42	14	40	12	Dresses
44	16	42	14	Dresses
46	18	44	16	Dresses
38	4.5	38	6	Shoes
38	5	38	6.5	Shoes
39	5.5	39	7	Shoes
39	6	39	7.5	Shoes
40	6.5	40	8	Shoes
41	7	41	8.5	Shoes

WHEN DEPARTING

- Airport departure tax is added to the price of your ticket at the time of purchase.
- It is forbidden to export antiquities and works of art found in Greece.
- Allowances for exporting other goods vary with the destination – check before departure.
- Reconfirm your flight times the day before departure.

LANGUAGE

The Greek language has an alphabet of its own, and the sounds are not particularly easy for the English speaker. As a visitor to Greece, you will find it helpful to know the Greek alphabet so that you can recognise placenames, as romanised spellings can vary. Some useful words and phrases have been listed phonetically below, the stresses marked with an accute accent. More extensive coverage can be found in the AA *Essential Greek Phrase Book* which contains over 2,000 words and 2,000 phrases.

guest house	*i pansyón*	shower	*to doos*
single room	*to monó dhomátyo*	towel	*i petséta*
double room	*to dhipló dhomátyo*	room service	*To dhomatíoo/ room sérvis*
bed	*to kreváti*	chambermaid	*i kamaryéra*
toilet (bathroom)	*i twaléta*	key	*to klidhí*
toilet paper	*to charti iyías*	a lift	*to asansér*
bath	*to bányo*	cockroaches	*katsarídhes*

bank	*i trápeza*	money	*ta leftá*
post office	*to tahidhrómio*	how much?	*póso káni*
exchange office	*to kanéna ghrafio*	exchange rate	*i isotimía*
post box	*to ghrama-tokivótyo*	I'd like to change some money	*tha ithela naláxo chrímata*
travellers' cheque	*i taxidhyotikí epitayí*	can I pay by...	*boró na plíroso me...*
credit card	*i pistotikí kárta*	cheap/expensive	*ftinós/akrivós*

restaurant	*to estiatório*	menu	*to menóo o katáloghos*
table	*to trapézi*		
tea (black)	*to tsái*	waiter	*to garsóni*
coffee	*o kafés*	waitress	*i servitóra*
milk	*to ghála*	wine	*to krasí*
beer	*i bira*	dessert	*to epidhórpyo*
water	*to neró*	fruit	*to fróoto*
bread	*to psomí*	bill	*o loghariazmós*

bus	*to leofório*	petrol	*i venzíni*
car	*to aftokínito*	petrol station	*venzinádhiko*
taxi	*to taxí*	car trouble	*i vlávi*
train	*to tréno*	ticket	*to isitírio*
airport	*to aerodhrómio*	single ticket	*apló isitírio*
aircraft	*to aeropláno*	return ticket	*metepistrofís*
ferry	*to féribot*	no smoking	*mi kapnízondes*
port/harbour	*to limáni*	timetable	*to dhromolóyo*

hello	*yásas, yásoo*	excuse me	*me sinchoríte*
good morning	*kaliméra*	child	*to pedhí*
good evening	*kalispéra*	goodbye	*yásas, yásoo*
yes	*ne*	doctor	*o yatrós*
no	*óhi*	I'm ill	*ime árostos/ árosti*
please	*parakaló*		
thank you	*efcharistó*	police	*i astinomía*
how are you?	*ti kánete?*	today	*símera*
very well	*polí kalá*	tomorrow	*ávrio*
you're welcome	*parakaló*	closed	*klistós*
I'm sorry	*lipáme*	open	*anichtós*

INDEX

INDEX

Acknowledgements
The Automobile Assocation wishes to thank the following photographers, libraries and organisations for their assistance in the preparation of this book:

EMBASSY OF GREECE 122a; GREEK ARCHAEOLOGICAL SERVICE 79; JUST GREECE PHOTO LIBRARY 12, 27b, 41b; MARY EVANS PICTURE LIBRARY 11, 14; MIKE GERRARD 48, 74; MINISTRY OF CULTURE 8a; MRI BANKERS' GUIDE TO FOREIGN CURRENCY 119; NATIONAL ARCHAEOLOGICAL MUSEUM 15b; PICTURES COLOUR LIBRARY 117a; SPECTRUM COLOUR LIBRARY Cover Parthenón, 27a, 62, 64, 65, 66, 71, 75, 76, 90; WORLD PICTURES LTD 6, 28/9, 67, 70/1, 78, 80/1; ZEFA PICTURES LTD 9b, 28, 63, 70, 82.

The remaining transparencies are held in the Association's own library (AA PHOTO LIBRARY) with contributions from Steve Day 122b, 122c; T Harris 1, 5a, 5b, 7, 9a, 13, 15a, 16a, 16b, 19, 20, 23a, 23b, 25, 40, 41a, 43, 46, 49, 52/3, 54, 55, 56, 57a, 57b, 58, 59, 60, 86, 88, 91b, 117b; R Surman 18/19, 22, 24, 26, 29, 32, 35, 44, 45, 47, 51, 53, 57b, 61, 69, 72, 84, 85, 87a, 87b, 89; P Wilson 2, 8b, 9c, 17, 21, 30, 31, 33, 34, 36, 37, 38, 39, 42, 91a.

Mike Gerrard wishes to thank Panos Argyros and his assistant Claire Carroll, both at the National Tourist Organisation of Greece, for their invaluable help.

Contributors
Verifier: Pip Leahy Researcher (Practical Matters): Lesley Allard
Indexer: Marie Lorimer

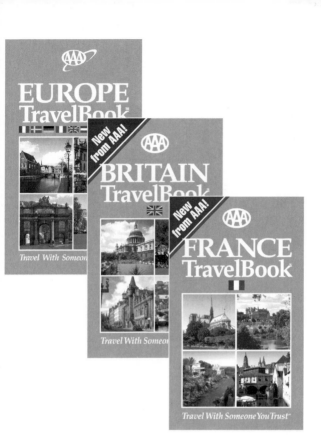

AAA EUROPE TRAVELBOOK SERIES

EUROPE □ BRITAIN □ FRANCE

This exclusive TravelBook series offers everything needed
when traveling through Europe, France, or Britain. Packed
with pages of sightseeing information, full-color maps,
driving tours, customs regulations and more!

Available through your local AAA office.

AAA ROAD ATLAS SERIES

EUROPE □ BRITAIN □ FRANCE

This series of detailed road atlases offers travelers everything needed for touring Europe, Britain, or France. Each atlas features detailed maps of countries and cities, distance and mileage charts, metric conversion tables and much more!

Available through your local AAA office.